SPANISH *for* GRINGOS

LEVEL 1
Shortcuts, Tips, and Secrets to Successful Learning

Third Edition

William C. Harvey, M.S.

Illustrated
by
Paul Meisel

D1613841

BARRON'S

For all the gringos who try ...

grin-go \ 'grin-(,) gō\ *n, pl* **gringos** [Sp, alter. of *griego* Greek, stranger, fr. L *Graecus* Greek] (1849): a foreigner in Spain or Latin America esp. when of English or American origin ...

By permission. From Webster's 11th New Collegiate Dictionary © 2003 by Merriam-Webster Inc., publisher of the Merriam-Webster dictionaries.

About the Author

William C. Harvey is founder of Language Services Institute, a highly-successful conversational Spanish program aimed specifically at meeting the needs of today's busy adult learner. For the past 20 years he has taught Spanish and ESL (English as a Second Language) in school districts and community colleges, as well as in private industry. He has also traveled extensively throughout the West Coast giving workshops and seminars to teachers and professional organizations. Mr. Harvey holds a bachelor's degree in Spanish and a master's degree in Bilingual-Bicultural Education from Cal State University, Fullerton, where he received the "Project of the Year" award for his work in ESL Curriculum Development. Bill has written several books for Barron's, including *Spanish for Law Enforcement, Household Spanish, Spanish for Healthcare Professionals,* and *Spanish for Educators.*

All inquiries should be addressed to:
Barron's Educational Series, Inc.
250 Wireless Boulevard
Hauppauge, NY 11788
http://www.barronseduc.com

ISBN-13: 978-0-7641-3951-2 (book only)
ISBN-10: 0-7641-3951-7 (book only)
ISBN-13: 978-0-7641-9460-3
ISBN-10: 0-7641-9460-7

Library of Congress Catalog Card No. 2008923155

Printed in the United States of America
9 8

10%
POST-CONSUMER WASTE
Paper contains a minimum of 10% post-consumer waste (PCW). Paper used in this book was derived from certified, sustainable forestlands.

CONTENTS

Hola, **fellow gringos!**

Finally, after years of teaching classroom Spanish using the dreadful "textbook approach," I got fed up and decided to try something different. Having picked up Spanish myself by hanging around non-English speakers, I'd discovered what gringos *really* needed to learn *el español.* So I put together a series of practical, easy-to-follow shortcuts, tips, and secrets to success—designed specifically for folks who aren't interested in "studying" a foreign language. In place of traditional units and lessons, *Spanish for Gringos* is intended as a guidebook and offers nothing more than helpful suggestions. This approach should make your language learning experience easy and *muy divertido* (lots of fun)!

Adiós for now,

Bill

Reasons Why Spanish Is Easy to Learn

Other languages are great, but believe me—I've chosen Spanish because it is the easiest of them all. I've spent my life developing *Spanish for Gringos* for six very good reasons.

1   Spanish is a lot like English.

Most Spanish words have the same Latin-based form as their English equivalents. Many words in both languages look and sound almost the same, which makes guessing a breeze.

2   Spanish is not complicated.

Conversations in Spanish can be kept short and sweet. Complex messages are often exchanged using only a few simple words. Only an understanding of basic grammar and pronunciation patterns is needed for successful communication to take place.

3   It's OK if you blow it.

Spanish speakers enjoy helping gringos who try. Hispanics are generally proud, warm-hearted people who admire those with a sincere interest in learning their native tongue. So cheer up. Lousy Spanish only makes *you* feel stupid.

4   Spanish is not hard to practice.

All across the nation, the Hispanic population continues to grow at a tremendous rate. Regular exposure to Spanish should not be a major problem. Neither should it be difficult for the learner to find someone to "practice with." Also remember that lots of Spanish still lies just south of the border.

5   Spanish can be profitable.

American business people have discovered that buying and selling in more than one language makes good business sense. And with Hispanics in the United States now spending millions a day, their market has become a primary target of corporate America. Increasingly, companies are providing Spanish training for employees. And better pay seems to make learning that much easier. So revise that résumé! Learning Spanish can lead to financial success.

6   Spanish is fun to learn.

There's nothing like the thrill of speaking Spanish and being understood for the first time. Or the *second* time. It's not long before gringos get "hooked." Maybe it's because communication in a new language allows you to meet, understand, and assist more people. That does wonders for the self-image. Spanish also can make life more fun. In traveling to Spanish-speaking countries, common activities such as shopping and dining suddenly become more enjoyable and exciting. A second language is like a new toy—so play with it! After mastering Spanish you will find that similar languages, like French and Italian, are easier to learn. And don't worry about staying motivated. It seems that once gringos get rolling in *español*, they're usually very difficult to stop!

"Who Needs It?"

Spanish for Gringos is not for everyone.

For those of you who plan on living in Spain or Latin America and need extensive language training ... I'm sorry. And to those who already speak Spanish and are looking to improve their reading and writing skills ... I apologize. You see, this guidebook was *not* written for people whose intentions are to "study."

Spanish for Gringos is for everybody else.

Most of what you'll find here is basic, practical information that you can use right away, with a lot of the technical "stuff" trimmed away. Generalizations about Spanish are made. Translations are not "precise." And the primary theme is to *assist gringos only*, as they begin communication with Spanish speakers at work or at play.

Although this guidebook should help any Spanish learners, it is basically *an orientation to the type of Spanish that is commonly spoken here in the United States.*

Before You Begin

OK, *brace yourselves!* This guidebook contains *no* drills, *no* worksheets, and *no* tests!

… Instead, learners will be asked to follow some
RATHER UNUSUAL GUIDELINES

- **Forget what you've been told!** (You'll just get hung-up on useless details.) There's no such thing as perfect Spanish, so don't get stuck trying to figure out the best way to say something. This book gives you only what you *need* to know. Instead of traditional grammar and pronunciation practice, try the practical shortcuts, tips, and secrets to success. If you follow the useful suggestions, you'll be all right most of the time.

- **Spend most of your time listening!** (You'll be talking in no time.) To learn the way a baby learns language, it's important to "take in" lots of Spanish at the beginning. Listen to fluent speakers. Soon, new words will emerge naturally in everyday conversation. Use the one-liners and greetings freely, but don't force speech until you feel ready to speak. On-line language programs, DVDs, and interactive CDs can be helpful. But real-life practice is better!

- **Act as if you know more than you do!** (You'll soon believe that you *are* fluent.) Learn to have self-confidence around people who speak only Spanish. Even if you don't understand a word, smile and laugh a lot. "Concentrate" when you are asked a question, and always answer with a short response. Imitate verbal and nonverbal expressions. Be assertive, yet remain friendly. Experiment with new words and phrases. Fake it, and you'll be speaking Spanish *pronto!*

- **Don't make excuses!** (You'll never get started if you do.) Thanks to modern research, we now know that the following statements about language learning are Untrue!

You need to do grammar exercises . . . . *No!*
You need to develop good pronunciation . . . . *No!*
You need to start at an early age . . . . *No!*
You need to memorize vocabulary lists . . . . *No!*
You need to be "good at languages" . . . . *No!*

So there! The truth is you have *no excuse* and ...
You *will* learn Spanish quickly and easily . . . . *Sí!*

- **Most of all, relax!** The idea of learning a new language scares the life out of most people, so don't feel ashamed. Just accept the fact that you're going to sound strange and look awkward for a while. It's no big deal. This guidebook is designed to relieve you of stress and frustration. Never give up! Don't worry about a thing, have some fun, and just go for it. With *Spanish for Gringos* learning *no es problema.*

Checklist

1	**Comfortable chair**	☐
2	**Background music**	☐
3	**Favorite beverage**	☐
4	**Laid-back attitude**	☐

1

CHAPTER *UNO*

¿Habla español?

(Do You Speak Spanish?)

Spanish Words Most Gringos Already Know:

americano	cerveza
amigo	margarita
amor	tequila
español	vino
se habla inglés	
loco	bueno
macho	grande
padre	mucho
plaza	más
pueblo	
rancho	adiós
señor	gracias
señorita	Feliz Navidad
	hasta la vista
fiesta	por favor
cha-cha-cha	pronto
el tango	sí
olé	
	dinero
burrito	uno
chile	dos
enchilada	tres
salsa	
taco	Lambada
	cucaracha
latino	no problema
gringo	Los Angeles
chiquita	bandido
zorro	bravo

Spanglish

A unique blend of Spanish and English has gradually evolved in the United States as more and more Spanish speakers and English speakers have made attempts to communicate. Nationwide, Spanglish is alive and well (though words may vary from region to region). You see, many English words either can't be exactly translated into Spanish or are just easier to say when mixed with English. What's great is that they all sound like words gringos know. Check out these easy-to-remember "Spanish Englishisms":

NOTE
Spanglish is not street slang! But it's *not Spanish*, either. So some people may make comments. Be prepared!

SPANGLISH	ENGLISH	SPANISH
bloquear	to block	*obstruir*
cachar	to catch	*coger*
chequear	to check	*revisar*
craquear	to crack	*romper*
cuitiar	to quit	*renunciar*
lonchar	to lunch	*almorzar*
parquear	to park	*estacionar*
taipiar	to type	*escribir a máquina*
wachar	to watch	*mirar*

Did you know? Mixing both languages when "you can't remember" is still OK!

HOT TIP!

If it's close—they'll probably get it! Since Spanglish and English are so similar, you really don't need to worry about pronunciation.

SPANGLISH	ENGLISH	SPANISH
la baika	bike	*la bicicleta*
las brekas	brakes	*los frenos*
la carpeta	carpet	*la alfombra*
el lonche	lunch	*el almuerzo*
la marqueta	market	*el mercado*
el mofle	muffler	*el silenciador*
el pay	pie	*el pastel*
el raite	ride	*un paseo*
la troca	truck	*el camión*
la yarda	yard	*el patio*

> **NOTE**
> Don't struggle with the pronunciation of Spanish words yet! You'll be getting the "Secrets to Soundmaking" shortly.

HOT TIP!

Are you aware that names of people, cities, streets, buildings, companies, and brand names are *not* usually translated into Spanish?

la IBM   los Levis
el Hilton   el Kleenex
los Pampers   la Budweiser

Vamos a Chicago.   Let's go to Chicago.
El señor Iglesias habla español.   Mister Iglesias speaks Spanish.
Trabajo en el Marriott.   I work at the Marriott.

Understanding Spanish Speakers

You're right. It does sound like one long word. Everything is too fast. So what's a gringo to do? Well, don't panic. Relax, smile, and try these **Five Secrets to Success:**

1 Focus on the message.

Listen for key words and how they're expressed, instead of trying to understand *the whole enchilada.* Are they asking or telling you something? Avoid translating each word. Concentrate on the main idea only.

2 Use your hands and face.

Express comprehension by pointing, moving, or touching things. Make faces. Write or draw what you think they're trying to say. Be as expressive as you can. Soon, they'll get into the act. Don't give up, and you'll eventually end up communicating with *no problemas.*

3 Say: *Más despacio, por favor.*

(Mahs des-pah´-syo, por fah-bo´r) which means: "More slowly please." Or say *¿Qué?* (kay) and *¿Cómo?* (ko´mo) which mean "What?" and "How's that?"

4 Listen for the English.

Since both languages are Latin based, many Spanish words sound a lot like English. Guess and you'll probably be right!

5 Relax and try again.

Swallow your pride and remember—they're having as much trouble as you are. Lighten up, believe in yourself, and *español* will begin to make sense.

Hey, Listen!
(¡Escuche!)

Don't say a word! You don't have to. Much like children learn their native tongue, it's best to *listen first!* So don't force yourself to speak. After listening to Spanish for a while, *it will gradually start coming out of you!* For now, try some of these easy (and inexpensive) ways to pick up on those new "foreign noises":

- Listen to Spanish radio stations (check local listings).
- Find out which TV stations also air in Spanish.
- Watch Spanish movies (with English subtitles).
- Search for Spanish downloads, podcasts, and video clips.
- Ride city buses or subways through Spanish-speaking areas.
- See a Spanish language play or musical performance.
- Attend a Spanish-speaking religious service of your faith.
- Join a Spanish-speaking club, team, or organization.
- Check into travel packages to Spain or Latin America.
- Befriend those Spanish speakers whom you see regularly.
- Take a Spanish class, or buy a program with lots of on-line practice!

HOT TIP!

You can obviously add your own ideas to this list. But however you choose to *escuchar* (listen), always remember the three **C**s: **C**alm down, Observe **C**losely, and **C**oncentrate on what's being said!

The "Nonverbals"

Guess what? If you'd like to communicate in Spanish, but don't feel like speaking, there's an easy and fun way to send messages. As with most cultures, certain *hand signals, facial expressions,* and *body language* convey valuable meaning. Here are some of my favorite hand signals from Mexico.

I love it! Talk without speaking!

Venga.
Come here.

By moving your hand (or arm) in a downward motion, you're calling someone to you.

Un momento.
Just a moment.

By putting your thumb and index finger together, you're telling someone, "Hold on just a moment. I'll be right with you."

No gracias.
No thanks.

By moving your pointer finger back and forth, you're telling someone "No" or "Don't."

More nonverbals

Touching your elbow while looking at folks is the same as calling them tightwads or "cheap."

NOTE
If you know how to say the words, add them for emphasis.

¡*Ojo!*
Beware!

Pointing to your eye means "Be careful" or "Watch out!"

¡*Qué grande!*
How big!

Always point upwards, with palm side of the hand toward you, when referring to the height of a person …

… and outwards, palm-side-down, when referring to the height of an object or animals.

NOTE
There are many more, so take time to observe people as they interact. Ask the meanings if you're not sure. Practice the nonverbals and you'll be able to "communicate" right away!

¿Puede recordarlo?
Can You Remember It?

I know we have just begun, but why not stop and review a moment before moving on to the next chapter. Just answer as many questions as you can!

- Give at least two reasons why Spanish is easy to learn.
- Which are some of the guidelines to learn Spanish quickly?
- Name five Spanish words you knew before reading this book.
- What is *Spanglish?*
- How can you get folks to slow down when they are speaking very fast?
- List two activities that can help you practice listening to Spanish.
- Give a "hand signal" in Spanish.

2

CHAPTER *DOS*

Las primeras palabras

(The First Words)

Secrets to Soundmaking

Basically, you need to know only *five* primary Spanish sounds that will make you comprehensible and help you to understand more. When speaking Spanish, if you make the following sounds every time the corresponding letter appears, you'll sound just like a native speaker. When? *Every time the letter appears!* Try making these sounds toward the front of your mouth instead of the back—with little or no air coming out. Short choppy sounds are better than long stretched-out ones. Go ahead, practice now that nobody's listening and soon you will be able to impress your friends.

Trust me! Know these and you will be on your way!

a (ah)	like y**a**cht
e (eh)	like m**e**t
i (ee)	like k**ee**p
o (oh)	like **o**pen
u (oo)	like sp**oo**n

HOT TIP!

Exactness doesn't matter! As I said before—if it's close, they'll probably get it. Besides, the goal of this guidebook is getting people to communicate, *not* teaching all the different Spanish sounds. So stop fretting. You sound great to me!

The Big Five

a   *banana, La Bamba, cha-cha-cha, mañana*
e   *tres, excelente, olé, elefante, nene*
i   *sí, dividir, Trini, Miami, Lidia*
o   *loco, ocho, no, colorado, dos*
u   *Lulú, mucho, tú, burro, Uruguay*

The "Others"

Easy enough. But what about the *other* sounds in Spanish? Good news—they're not much different from English. But here are a few that may cause confusion.

c has two sounds: **c**^{1} like **c**at and **c**^{2} like **c**elery, when followed by **e** or **i**. *g* also has two sounds: **g**^{1} (g) like **g**o and **g**^{2} (h) like **h**ello, when followed by **e** or **i**.

h   (*Don't* pronounce it; like **k** in knife.)
j (h)   like **h**ot
ll (y)   like **y**es
ñ (ny)   like ca**ny**on
qu (k)   like **k**iss
v (b)   like **b**reak
z (s)   like **s**it

More volume!
I can't hear you.

- Like the Big Five, these sounds have *no exceptions!* In Spanish, respective sounds are always the same *every time their corresponding letter appears!*
- Don't worry about your "regional accent." Making yourself understood in Spanish doesn't depend on what part of the United States *you* are from.

Now, let's try to put all these "pieces of noise" together. Refer back to the Secrets to Soundmaking as you read the following (**ALOUD**):

HOT TIPS!

- These 8 are the only "toughies." The rest can be pronounced the *same as English!*
- Take note! Gringos have the most trouble with *qu*.

c^1 *coco, carro, colorado, capitán*
c^2 *Cecilia, cigarro, centro, cilantro*
g^1 *gorila, garaje, guacamole, Paraguay*
g^2 *general, Geraldo, gimnasio, rígido*
h *huevo, hombre, hola, ahora*
j *Juan, trabajo, frijoles, Julio*
ll *llama, millón, tortillas, amarillo*
$ñ$ *señor, mañana, español, piña colada*
qu *poquito, qué pasa, tequila, quesadilla*
v *vino, Victoria, viva, hasta la vista*
z *López, cerveza, Venezuela, González*

Here's a great way to practice some of your new Spanish sounds. Simply read each word aloud, and look up their meanings in English later on:

SOUNDS	PRONOUNCED	PRACTICE WORDS		
que	keh	*pequeño*	*porque*	*queso*
qui	kee	*chiquito* *máquina*	*quiero* *parquímetro*	*quién* *mosquito*
ji or *gi*	hee	*jinete* *girasol*	*gigante* *tejido*	*jirafa* *rugido*
je or *ge*	heh	*gemelos* *objeto*	*jefe* *tijeras*	*gente* *jeringa*
gue	geh	*guerra*	*manguera*	*juguete*
gui	ghee	*guitarra* *águila*	*guisantes* *alguien*	*seguir* *amiguito*
ce	seh	*cebolla*	*ceja*	*cárcel*
ci	see	*cine*	*capacidad*	*cocido*
lle	yeh	*lleno*	*ballena*	*calle*
lli	yee	*trillizos*	*allí*	*pollito*
lla	yah	*silla*	*olla*	*llamar*
llo	yoh	*bello*	*llorar*	*sillón*
llu	yoo	*lluvia*	*velludo*	

HOT TIPS!

- Always try to "visualize" Spanish words because they're spelled exactly as you say them. And **don't worry about what you sound like!**
- **Run 'em- together …** What's really nice about the *español* is that it's put together in little pieces—just like the *inglés*. So, to sound like a native speaker, **thefasterthebetter!**
- **Read 'em Right!** By now, you've probably noticed the little accent mark (´) on parts of certain words. Don't get nervous. It only means that you're supposed to say that part of the word **LOUDER!**

*Ma-**rí**-a*

Forget about the accent mark on little words, like *sí* or *qué!* That's just how they're spelled!

¡ANUNCIO IMPORTANTE!

Once you become familiar with the different Spanish sounds you'll make the *first giant step toward fluency!* So why not go back and read it again!

Más Pronunciation Details!

- If there's *no* accent mark, say the *last part* of the word louder (espa**ñol**).
- For words ending in the Big Five, *n* or *s,* the *second to the last* part of the word is emphasized (enchi**la**da).
- With **rr**, roll your Rs—but *only* if you can. They'll understand if you use **r** instead.
- The **d** sometimes sounds like our "th" (as in "this") in the middle and at the end of words. Try it: nada, todo, adiós
- People from Spanish-speaking countries don't all sound alike, but they all understand one another and will understand you.
- Forget "rules." They'll only make it worse!

> **NOTE**
> You won't find any more pronunciation "guides" next to words in this book. Instead, learn the "Secrets to Soundmaking" and practice in "real-life" situations!

Spanish Words That Don't Need Translating

There are literally thousands of Spanish words that are easy to understand. All you have to do is focus on **the English within.**
No need to translate these:

Go ahead—
read each one aloud!

EASY

aplicación	*fotografía*	*persona*
béisbol	*importancia*	*policía*
café	*inteligente*	*posesión*
comercial	*interesante*	*posible*
conversación	*limón*	*refrigerador*
escuela	*millonario*	*teléfono*
especial	*minuto*	*televisión*
estúpido	*momento*	*turismo*
familia	*nervioso*	*universidad*
fantástico	*noviembre*	*vacación*
favorito	*operación*	*vocabulario*

The EASIEST

banana	*hockey*	*natural*
chocolate	*horrible*	*plaza*
color	*hospital*	*popular*
doctor	*hotel*	*radio*
final	*idea*	*taxi*
golf	*individual*	*terror*

Other Easy to Remember Words

diccionario	*instrumento*	*programa*
dieta	*moderno*	*presidente*
dólar	*música*	*reservación*
eléctrico	*producto*	*sincero*
elegante	*profesional*	*violento*
información	*sexo*	*restaurante*

Mi buena memoria (My good memory)
Start today! Make a *lista* of Spanish words (without looking back) that you already have "picked up." You'll be surprised.

_____

_____

_____

_____

_____

_____

_____

¡UNA NOTICIA IMPORTANTE!
"Add" an upside-down mark in front of
Exclamations and *Questions*

Do you understand?	*¿Comprende?*
Yes! I understand!	*¡Sí! ¡Yo comprendo!*

HOT TIPS!

- **Remember:** *No pain-no gain!* As in all stretching exercises, when you pronounce this stuff, *make it hurt! Use those "mouth muscles"!*
- **Spanish sounds a bit like English**—but with an accent!
- **Be careful!** Some Spanish words look like English—but aren't. For example, *contestar* (to answer) has nothing to do with contests. And *pan* (bread) or *pie* (foot) could cause confusion!

Speak Up! (¡Hable!)

¡Hola Ramón! ¿Qué pasa?

Yo...er... mumble... mumble... mumble...

Again: *Don't worry* about "sounding dumb." All that matters is that you some-how manage to *understand* each other!

Muchos Ways to Practicar

Listening to Spanish was no big deal. The next step, then, is to practice *saying* something. (Once you've warmed up with Spanish words that resemble English, try these practice techniques for improving pronunciation, while picking up the hard-to-remember stuff:)

- Next time you're at an Hispanic restaurant, order food for everyone at the table.
- Look up and read all the names under González in the phone book. Then do the same with Sánchez or García.
- Travel through Spanish-speaking sections of town and say aloud the words on billboards and store windows. (You may get funny looks!)
- Randomly open books on the Southwest, Latin America, or Spain, and try pronouncing all the Spanish words you find.
- Next time you're alone, try reading English aloud—but use the Spanish Secrets to Soundmaking! Don't laugh—it works!
- Start slowly. Try practicing *one sound a week!*
- Tape yourself regularly while reading Spanish language newspapers or magazines.
- If possible, buy some language DVDs or CDs and work with them.
- Get on the Internet and search for a Spanish-speaking "chatroom." Find out all the ways to interact on-line with your Spanish-speaking friends.

HOT TIP!

The best way to learn a new language is to talk face to face with someone. Think of convenient ways to learn Spanish from Hispanic people. One popular method is to offer a little English instruction in return.

Baby's First *Palabras* (Words)

We've already taken a look at *Words Gringos Already Know* and *Should Know*. Now it's time to try words and phrases you *have to know*. In the same way a baby learns "survival words" at first, it's best to start with the Spanish that will take you the farthest. The following seem to be the words acquired first in any language. Use them to communicate complete messages. (**Wait!** Check back on the Secrets to Soundmaking!)

agua	water
amigo	friend
baño	bathroom
bueno	good
carro	car
casa	house
comida	food
dinero	money
grande	big
hombre	man
más	more
mucho	a lot
mujer	woman
muy bien	very well
niño	child
nombre	name
número	number
persona	person
teléfono	phone
trabajo	work
por favor	please
gracias	thanks
hola	Hi!
adiós	Bye!

> Put two or more together!
> *y* = and
> *o* = or
> **pero** = but
> *¡Gracias y adiós!*

> These words are grasped early also: *Señor (Sr.)* is a "Mr."; *Señora (Sra.)* is a "Mrs."; *Señorita (Srta.)* is a "Miss." *Sorry*, there is no word for "Ms."—**yet**!

(So, how's your soundmaking?)

My Favorite First Words

Here are more gems that work all by themselves.

algo	something	*alguien*	someone
ahora mismo or *ahorita*	right now	*los demás*	the rest of them
después	afterwards	*ninguno*	none of them
antes	before	*cualquiera*	any of them
mientras	during	*cada uno*	each one
entonces	then	*ambos*	both of them
ya	already	*algunos*	some
demasiado	too much	*varios*	several
otra	another	*nada*	nothing
otra vez	again	*siguiente*	the next one
casi	almost	*mismo*	the same
juntos	together	*diferente*	different
solo	alone	*primero*	first
todo	all of it	*último*	last
nadie	no one	*en todas partes*	everywhere

HOT TIPS!

- To really impress, just greet with: *¡Buenos!* (daytime) or *¡Buenas!* (late afternoon and evening). *¡Hola!* Hi! and *¡Qué tal!* How's it going! can be used anytime.
- Instead of *Adiós* (Good-bye), try *Nos vemos* (We'll see ya), or

Hasta (Until) { *luego* (later) *mañana* (tomorrow) *la vista* (next time) }

- Find some more and have fun!

The Greetings and Stuff

Having any problems in getting started? Your troubles are over. Memorize these as one long word and they'll think you're fluent!

Buenos días.   Good morning

Buenas tardes.   Good afternoon

Buenas noches.   Good evening or Good night

More Courtesies

"Hello?"

¿Aló?, ¿Bueno? or *¿Diga?* are all good when you answer the phone. "Who's calling?" is *¿De parte de quién?*

"Who's There?"

When you knock and want to enter, it's *¿Se puede?* (Can I come in?). To say "Come in!" use: *¡Pase!* or *¡Adelante!*

"Thanks!"

Instead of the old, *Muchas gracias* for "Thanks a lot," try these stronger words of appreci-ation: **¡Muchísimas gracias! ¡Mil gracias!** or the one I use: **¡Muy amable!** "very friendly"

Por favor is "please."
De nada is "you're welcome."
Lo siento is "I'm sorry."

> Remember that Spanish speakers exchange greetings regularly. Try learning other ways folks say hello, and don't be afraid to "greet" someone back!

¿Se puede?

"Excuse Me!"

Whenever you'd like to get through a crowd, use *¡Con permiso!* If you cough or sneeze, say: *¡Perdón!* To get someone's attention, try: *¡Disculpe! ¡Pase!* is "Go ahead!" *¡Salud!* is "Bless you!"

 vs.

¿Qué pasa?

This is the standard "What's happening?" Sometimes you'll be greeted with *¿Qué ...* (and something else)? Don't worry! They're still only asking what's going on. Here's the easy way out: always answer with— *"¡Sin novedad!"* or *"¡Nada!"* (Nothing new!)

¿Cómo está usted?

Everyone knows this one. It means, "How are you?" And as with *¿Qué pasa?*, when you hear, *¿Cómo ...* (something)? you can "sneak by" using the classic, *¡Muy bien!* (Just fine!)

> **NOTE**
> Later on, we'll take a look at other ways to answer these *¿Qué ...?* and *¿Cómo ...?* questions.

Las presentaciones
(Introductions)

There are many ways to say, "Nice to meet you!" but the most common is *¡Mucho gusto!* During the introduction, don't forget to shake the other person's hand. If something is said to *you* first, smile and say, *¡igualmente!*, which translates to, "Same to you."

   ¿Cómo se llama? (What's your name?) and *Me llamo* _____. (My name is _____). are also nice to know!

¿Dónde está?
(Where is it?)

More than likely, the very first question you'll get asked will be, "Where's the bathroom?" (Whenever anyone needs directions, they'll use, *¿Dónde está...?*) Here, then, is what you'll need:

... *a la derecha* = to the right
... *a la izquierda* = to the left
... *adelante* or *derecho* = straight ahead
... *aquí* or *acá* = here
... *ahí* = there
... *allá* = over there

¡Viva el vocabulario! (Long Live Vocabulary!)

Following are three groups of words most folks seem to pick up and use almost immediately.

Los números
(The numbers)
0   *cero*
1   *uno*
2   *dos*
3   *tres*
4   *cuatro*
5   *cinco*
6   *seis*
7   *siete*
8   *ocho*
9   *nueve*

Los colores
(The colors)
black   *negro*
blue   *azul*
brown   *café*
gray   *gris*
green   *verde*
orange *anaranjado*
purple *morado*
red   *rojo*
white   *blanco*
yellow *amarillo*

La clase
(The class)

el libro

el lápiz

la pluma

el papel

el cuaderno

la mesa

la computadora

la impresora

el escritorio

la silla

HOT TIPS!

- More numbers will be introduced later. Can you say the preceding numbers with your eyes closed?
- "Look up" more colors if you need others. And learn by "word-picture association." For example, *BLANK* white paper is *blanco*. (How clever can you be?)
- More new words are on their way. For now, go find these things around you. Touch them and name them in *español*—and no cheating!

CHOOSE 'n USE Here are some sentences that will help you put these words to practice. Fill in the blanks, read each sentence aloud, and plan ways to use them in real-life situations.

- **Los números**

  Mi número de teléfono es …   My telephone number is … (542-8763, etc.).

  ¿Dónde está el cuarto número …?   Where's room number … (five, three, etc.)?

- **Los colores**

  Me gusta el color …   I like the color … (purple, red, etc.).
  ¿Es … o …?   Is it … (black, etc.) or … (white, etc.)?
  Hay algunos de color …   There are some … (orange, etc.) ones.

- **La clase**

  ¿Tiene usted un/una …   Do you have a … (pen, book, etc.)?

  … está en …   The … (paper, notebook, etc.) is "in," "on," or "at" the … (desk, table, etc.).

  Necesito …   I need the … (computer, chair, etc.).

At the end of this book you'll discover a Personal Success Chart. Use it! Simply pencil in your "experiences." Try out your new skills regularly. See how fast your **lista** can grow!

¿Puede recordarlo? (Can You Remember It?)

- Pronounce the five vowels in Spanish (The Big Five!).
- Write three Spanish words that are spelled the same in English.
- Name one way you plan to practice "speaking" Spanish.
- Give one expression in Spanish that is used to greet someone.
- Say the numbers 1 through 9 in Spanish.

3

CHAPTER *TRES*
Más, Más, Más
(More, More, More)

This is how you say "The."

The *El* and *La* Business

If you want to name a single object or person, put either *el* (masculine) or *la* (feminine) in front. It may seem strange, but as you continue to learn more *español*, you will need to know the meanings of "masculine" and "feminine." In Spanish, single objects require either an *el* or a *la* in front. This has nothing to do with an object's sex! It's just the *el* and *la* Business! In order to remember which one to use, just check to see if the word ends in either an *o* (generally masculine) or an *a* (generally feminine).

el

el ta**c**o
el ami**g**o
el bur**r**o

HOT TIPS!

- A few words are weird (**i.e.,** *el sofá, la mano, el problema*).
- Some words don't end in **o** or **a** (**i.e.,** *el elefante, la paz*)
- *El* and *la* refer not only to male and female persons (**i.e.,** *el señor, la dama*), but to animals as well.
- *It doesn't matter* if you get confused and use the wrong one, *you'll still be understood!* So don't hold back!

la

la enchilad**a**
la señori**ta**
la cucarach**a**

More *El/La* Business and *Un/Una*

The following are common questions and answers about one part of Spanish that is completely foreign to English.

1 Can *el* and *la* also refer to more than one person, animal or thing?

No way, José. Two or more *tacos* and *enchiladas* become:

los *tacos* and **las** *enchiladas*

> Notice what happens to *el*. More than *uno* is *los*.
>
> See? You've got to tag on the "s" at the end.

2 How do I say "a" or "an" instead of "the"?

At times in English we use "a" or "an" to say "any old thing." In Spanish, use **un** or **una**:

un *taco* and **una** *enchilada* are "a" taco and "an" enchilada.

> And guess what? **Unos** and **unas** mean "some."

3 Why is this aspect of Spanish a little confusing?

The answer is simple: You're not used to it yet! Grasping these concepts may take a little time. Besides, your messing up Spanish won't make much difference! Your listeners will figure out what you said anyway. But if you do "get corrected" just say to yourself—"I'll get it right the next time!"

HOT TIPS!

- Words (naming things, people, or concepts) that have the following endings, *usually* need *la* (feminine) in front.
  = *a*
  = *sión*
  = *tad*
  = *ción*
  = *dad*
  = *umbre*
  = *ambre*
- Textbooks call this *masculine* and *feminine gender*.
- By the way, *él*, with an accent mark means "he."
- *uno* is "one" also!
- Talking about "more than one" (plurals) is a lot like *inglés*:
  cuatro tacos
  four tacos
  cinco relojes
  five watches

The Once-and-for-All Rule

- You can expect to get the hang of this *rápido!*
- Matching the **o**'s and **a**'s works great with *"Los colores"!*:
  Muchos carros blancos Many white cars;
  muchas casas blancas.
  But: *muchos carros azules*

As we've learned, talking about "more than one" (plural) in Spanish is very much as it is in English; (**un** *taco* → **dos** *tacos*). Words not ending in the Big Five take **es** at the end; **un** *doctor* → **dos** *doctores*).

What isn't like English is what I call the "Once-and-for-all Rule." You see, not only do all Spanish words that name (nouns) or describe (adjectives) things, people, or concepts need "s," or "es" to make them plural but when they are used together, the **o**'s and **a**'s (masculine and feminine) must match.

Muchos tacos   Many tacos
y and
Muchas enchiladas   Many enchiladas

NOTA IMPORTANTE

Muchos means "many."
Mucho means "a great deal" or "a lot." ... And don't confuse *mucho* with *muy*, which means "very."

poco a little bit   *poquito* a very little bit
pocos a few   *poquitos* very few

Did you notice?
= *ito* and = *ita* word endings reduce things.

The "One-a-Day" One-liners

A very good way to gain confidence while learning a new language is to speak in short, meaningful phrases. Instead of struggling with the formation of correct long sentences, expressive one-liners can be used— especially when there's really nothing left to say. And using them will make you feel more confident! You'll sound more fluent than you actually are. Practice a new one every day … (Careful! They're addictive!)

Use these phrases whenever you think it might be appropriate.

¡Por supuesto!   Of course!
¡Quizás!   Maybe!
¡Me alegro!   I'm so glad!
¡Es verdad!   That's the truth!
¡Más o menos!   More or less!
¿Está bien?   Is that OK?
¡Creo que sí!   I think so!
¡Cómo no!   Why not!
¡Es posible!   It's possible!
¡Claro!   Sure!
¡De acuerdo!   I agree!
¡Sin duda!   No doubt!
¡Depende!   That depends!
¡A lo contrario!   On the contrary!

¡Buena idea!   Good idea!
¡Yo también!   Me, too!
¡Yo tampoco!   Me, neither!
¡Ojalá!   I hope so!
¡Ya veo!   I see!
¿Quién sabe?   Who knows?
¿Está seguro(a)?   Are you [he/she] sure?
¿Así?   Like this?
¡Lo que (usted) quiera!   Whatever you want!
¡Tanto mejor!   All the better!
¡Con razón!   No wonder!
¡Está bueno!   That's good!

For Busy *Personas*

¡Ya me voy!   I'm leaving now!
¡Ya se fue!   He or she has left!
¡Ahora vengo!   I'll be right back!
¡Ahí viene!   Here he or she comes!
¿Listo?   Ready?

HOT TIPS!

- Caution! Rudeness will ruin communication!
- These one-liners are great at *fiestas*! Here, for example, is a bit of one-liner dialogue.
Maria: *¿Listo?* (Ready?)
Carlos: *Creo que sí. ¿Y Tomás?* (I think so. And Thomas?)
Maria: *¡Ahí viene!* (Here he comes!)
Carlos: *¿Y Carolina?* (And Carolina?)
Maria: *¡Ya se fue!* (She's left!)
Carlos: *¡Está bueno!* (That's good!)

Más One-liners

No entiendo or *No comprendo.*
 I don't understand.
A la vez.   At the same time.
Muchas veces.   Lots of times.
Una vez.   One time.

No sé.   I don't know.

Todavía no.   Not yet.
Ahora no.   Not now.
En punto.   On time.

Al revés.   Backwards.
Boca abajo.   Upside down.

These expressions are often used instead of *adiós.*

¡Vaya con Dios!   Go with God!
¡Dios le bendiga!   God bless you!
¡Buen viaje!   Have a nice trip!
Me saluda a …   Give my regards to …
¡Tenga buen día!   Have a nice day!

Use these expressions, but with *emoción* (emotion)!

¡Felicitaciones!   Congratulations!
¡Feliz Navidad!   Merry Christmas!
¡Feliz cumpleaños!   Happy Birthday!

¡Socorro!   Help!
¡Caramba!   Wow!
¡Dios mío!   For heaven's sake!

¡Mentiras!   Lies!
¡Basta!   Enough!
¡Vaya!   Go on!
¡Vamos!   Let's go!
¡Buena suerte!   Good luck!

Es muy ...
It's very ...

cierto   certain
correcto   correct
fantástico   fantastic
importante   important
interesante   interesting
necesario   necessary
obvio   obvious
terrible   terrible

¡Qué ...

barbaridad!   How awful!
bueno!   How great!
chiste!   What a joke!
disfrute!   Have a good time!
extraño!   How strange!
lástima!   What a shame!
le vaya bien!   Take care!
se alivie!   Get well!
suerte!   What luck!
importa!   So what!
triste!   How sad!
va!   Pshaw, go on!

Embarrassed? Then go somewhere private and shut the door!

To learn even more one-liners, *listen carefully* and *ask* Spanish speakers what words and phrases mean! Repeat and practice alone until you *feel* prepared. Instead of writing these phrases, just memorize the sounds!

"Close Encounters"

If you've been paying attention, this will *not* be difficult. All you do is try to figure out what would be the best "natural" response. Write it only if you want to. Go ahead and use any of the words and phrases introduced so far.

Try more than one response. Check any previous page for possible responses. And, just as you would do in an actual situation—be creative!

Fantastic *Frases*

For the bravest of babblers, here are some "advanced plays" that truly make folks sound like they know what they're talking about.

Por eso ...	Therefore ...	*A propósito* ...	By the way ...
O sea ...	In other words ...	*Al principio* ...	At first ...
Además ...	Besides ...	*Por lo menos* ...	At least ...
Por fin ...	At last ...	*Según* ...	According to ...
Por ejemplo ...	For example ...	*En general* ...	In general ...
Sobre todo ...	Above all ...	*Paso a paso* ...	Step by step ...
Sin embargo ...	However ...	*Poco a poco* ...	Little by little ...

Here's an example of how it's done.

¿Mi carro? **En general,** *mi carro es excelente.*   My car? In general, my car is good.

Por ejemplo, *el color es perfecto.*   For example, the color is perfect.

Además, *es muy grande.*   Besides, it's very big.

Sin embargo, *el motor no es bueno.*   However, the engine isn't any good.

¿Mi carro? No sé.   My car? I don't know.

Now, you try it!

I Have a *Pregunta* (Question)

Suggestions for Success

Try to apply the following suggestions when making questions and giving answers in Spanish.

- **Focus on the first word!** There are only a few "question words," so learn them. The next step is to listen for main words in the question that you can recognize or "guess at." Concentrate on the "topic" of conversation.

- **Answer as briefly as possible!** Take your time. And if you want, repeat the question you've been asked. At first, only respond with key words and short phrases.

- **Relax and remember your English!** Whether you're asking or answering, try using each word just as you would in English. Again, it's OK to mix both languages if you should forget!

The Primary
Preguntas in *Español*

Make *muy* sure you can both understand and say the lifesaving *pregunta* words that follow:

¿Cuál?	What/Which?
¿Cómo?	How?
¿Qué?	What?
¿Dónde?	Where?
¿Cuánto?	How much?
¿Cuántos?	How many?
¿Cuándo?	When?
¿Quién?	Who?

HOT TIPS!

- All the *pregunta* words need accent marks. A few change meaning when you drop the accent: *como* (I eat) and *que* (that).
- Always put a "¿" at the beginning of a question, as well as the "?" at the end. **¿De acuerdo?**

¿Cuál ...? (What or which ...?)

Let's begin with the **cuál** questions; which can sometimes be answered with one or two words. Here are the most common questions needed to get basic information:

¿Cuál es su nombre?*   What is your name?   *Mi nombre es Juan.*
¿Cuál es su dirección?*   What's your address?   *Mi dirección es 363 Main St.*
¿Cuál es su número de teléfono?*   What's your phone number?   *Mi número es 555-1234.*
¿Cuál es su lugar de nacimiento?*   What's your place of birth?   *Mi lugar de nacimiento es La Habana.*

¿Cuál es su libro?*   Which (one) is your book?
¿Cuál es su lápiz?*   Which (one) is your pencil?
¿Cuál es su cuaderno?*   Which (one) is your notebook?
¿Cuál es su _____?*

- *¿Cuál?* all by itself means, "Which one?" *¿Cuáles?* means "Which one**s**" and is the word for "which" when there are *more than one*.

Make your own.

Nombre News (Juan, José, López, Pérez)

Keep in mind the following when you ask for a person's name.
- *¿Cómo se llama?* is another way to ask "What's your name?"
- *Primer nombre* is "first name."
- *Apellido* is "last name."

Juan   José
Primer nombre
(Not all Hispanic people have two first names!)

López
Apellido paterno
(Dad's)

Pérez
Apellido materno
(Mom's)

NOTES
- In the United States, this guy is just *Juan López*.
- When a woman marries, she keeps her dad's last name, followed by her husband's.
- There's no "middle name" as we know it.

HOT TIPS!

- **Slow down,** relax! Ask your questions and give your answers *palabra por palabra* (word by word), *letra por letra* (letter by letter), or *número por número* (number by number).
- *Su* means "his," "her," or "its" in addition to "your." SO POINT!
- *Qué* can also be used to mean, How …! *¡Qué grande!* How big!

¿Cómo?

All alone, *¿Cómo?* means *"What?"* or *"How's that?"* Use it like "How?" The classic *¿Cómo se llama?* literally means. "How are you called?" Now, can you tackle these other *cómo* concepts?

- *¿Cómo se dice?*   How do you say it?
- *¿Cómo se escribe?*   How do you write it?
- *¿Cómo está?*   How are you?

¿Qué?

¿Qué? always means "What?" as in *¿Qué pasa?* (What's happening?) Here are more *qué* classics:

Point to something and ask:
- *¿Qué es esto?*   What's this?

- *¿Qué es eso?*   What's that?
- *¿Qué son?*   What are they?
- *¿Qué significa?*   What does it mean?
- *¿Qué hora es?*   What time is it?

¿Dónde?

¿Dónde? is for direction; it is the "Where?" word. Whether you're looking for a person, place, or thing, just fill in the blank:

¿Dónde está   (Where's) ___?
"Look for" these phrases also:

¿Dónde vive?   Where do you live?

¿Dónde trabaja?   Where do you work?

¿Adónde va?   Where are you going?

¿De **dónde** es?   Where are you from?

¿Cuánto?

¿Cuánto(a)? (How much?) is the shopping word. *¿Cuántos(as)?* means "How many?" *Cuántos* applies to masculine nouns (*cuántos amigos*) and *cuántas* applies to feminine nouns (*cuántas amigas*). You can always "count" on these phrases:

¿Cuántos años tiene?   How old are you?

¿Cuánto tiempo?   How much time?

¿Cuánto cuesta?   How much does it cost?

¿Quién?

¿Quién es? means "Who is it?"

¿A **quién?** ...   To whom ...?

¿Quiénes son?   Who are they?

¿Para **quién?** ...   For whom ...?

¿De **quién?** ...   From whom ...?

NOTE
Words change a bit when you want to refer to *past* action. Don't be concerned! For now, use these as you would one-liners:
¿Cuándo nació? When were you born?
Fue ayer.   It was yesterday.
¿Qué pasó?   What happened?

¿Cuándo?

We'll be reading the clock and calendar soon, so let's warm up with some *¿Cuándo?* quickies.

¿Cuándo ...	*empieza?*	does it begin?
When ...	*termina?*	does it end?
	llega?	does it arrive?
	sale?	does it leave?
	nació usted?	were you born?

Long responses to these questions sound strange—so avoid using complex sentences. Keep those answers short!

¿Cuándo llega usted?—

Ayer.   Yesterday.
Hoy.   Today.
Mañana.   Tomorrow.

If you feel that you've had enough for now, take a break! Walk around, name things, or try out new words you've already learned. I'll be here when you get back!

Who's Who?

To really get going, you've got to know these important words, which can designate the **"who"** of a *quién(es)* question.

Use these words as you do their English equivalents and don't forget to point.

Yo   I

Usted   You

Ella   She

Él   He

Ellos   They

Ustedes   You guys

Nosotros   We

Note:
Ellas = "They," feminine;
Nosotras = "We," feminine.

HOT TIPS!

- The preceding *quién* words (subject pronouns) work wonderfully as one-word responses. Notice how they also "start you off" when expressing a complete message: *¿Quién es inteligente?—Ella es inteligente.* (Who is intelligent?—She is intelligent.)
- *Él, ella, ellos,* and *ellas* can refer to things as well as people: *Los libros, ¿dónde están ellos?* (The books, where are they?)
- "Grab onto" the first word in all questions, because they will make answering so much easier!

Posesión (Possession)

mi *amigo*
my friend

su *amigo*
their, your, his, or her friend

nuestro *amigo*
our friend

De él ...
De nosotros ...
De ellas ...

Just add "s" to both words (possessive adjective and noun) when talking about more than one.

- *mis amigos*
- *sus amigos*
- *nuestros amigos*

¿De quién es? (Whose is it?)

If someone (or something) "belongs to" someone else use *de* (of/from) to tell who the person is:

It's Maria's friend.

*Es el amigo **de** María.*

The *Posesión* Principles

- Don't forget the *El* and *La* Business:
  nuestra amiga   our friend

- Don't get possessive words (adjectives) mixed up with *quién* words (pronouns):
  *Yo tengo **mi** carro.*   **I** have **my** car.

- Try these possessive words once in a while:
  Es ...   mío.   mine.
  (It's)   *suyo.* yours, his, hers, *or* theirs.

- When you get stuck, escape with ***de!***
  ¿Es él un amigo   ***de ... usted?***   yours?
                      él?   his?
                      ella?   hers?
  Is he a friend **of** ***ellos?***   theirs (masculine)?
                      ellas?   theirs (feminine)?
                      ustedes?   yours?

- Perhaps you haven't noticed, but sometimes *en español*, it's OK to drop the *quién* word! It's already understood who's involved.
  *(yo) **Estoy** bien.*   **I'**m fine.

- A *very* important Spanish word is **tú**. It means "you," same as **usted**. However, while **usted** is used to address anybody *with respect*, **tú** is *informal* and is used with children, your family, or friends.

The Reversal Rule

In speaking Spanish, it is sometimes necessary to *think backwards!* For example, if you'd like to *describe* something, just *reverse* the order of the describing word and that of what's being described:

A lot of **good tacos.**
*Muchos **tacos buenos.***

… The same goes for *posesión*, Spanish first tells what belongs, then to whom it belongs:
John's house.
*La **casa** de **Juan.***

… As well as for giving addresses:
642 Broadway Avenue
Avenida Broadway 642

… In addition to some "action" words, which are sometimes reversed:
I like coffee.
Me gusta el café or *El café me gusta.*

… And many one-liners:
Not now!
¡Ahora no!

¡Entrevista!
(Interview!)

If you're truly serious about learning *español*, the *Entrevista* is for you. Here's how it works. Simply "prepare" three common questions and then write one in each top box to the right of the words *Los nombres* (names). See chart below. Next, go some place nearby where you can easily "interview" Spanish speakers. List their names under *Los nombres*. (To get their names, use Question 1.) *Fill in their responses* in the boxes to the right under each question.

Los nombres (Names)	*¿Cuál es su nombre?* (What's your name?)	*¿Cómo está usted?* (How are you?)	*¿De dónde es usted?* (Where are you from?)
José López	José	bien	Puerto Rico
María Sánchez			
Luis Pérez			

INFORMACIÓN IMPORTANTE

- The more Spanish you learn, the more "complex" your questions will become. No need to "force it" now.
- Spend time chatting with folks you interview. It's fun!
- Start slowly. Practice first with people you are familiar with.
- A three-question interview like this takes *less than 2 minutes* per person. "Too busy" is *no excuse!*
- If you should have trouble understanding, just have them "write-in" their own responses!
- Your approach should be friendly. Stop strangers with *"Disculpe."* ("Excuse me.") *"Estoy en un programa de español."* ("I'm in a Spanish program.") *"Quiero hacerle tres preguntas."* ("I want to ask you three questions.") *"Muchas gracias."* ("Thanks a lot.") Trust me. They'll *love* to help!

HOT TIPS!

- For the moment, use the *super-preguntas* just like a one-liner!
- The *super-preguntas* are even *more powerful* when other words are added. Take a chance and add words you already know:

  ¿Le gusta …   Do you like … (the wine, beer, etc.)?

  ¿Entiende usted … Do you understand … (English, the problem, etc.)?

  ¿Quisiera usted … Would you like (soda, coffee, etc.)?

  ¿Hay …   Are there a lot of … (people, books, etc.)?

  ¿Por qué …   Why don't you … (like it, etc.)?

  ¿Quiere usted …   Do you want … (more sauce, etc.)?

  ¿Tiene usted …   Do you have a … (car, good idea, etc.)?

- Once you "get" that first word, next try focusing on exactly what it is they are asking you!

The *Super-preguntas*

¿Cuál? _____
¿Cómo? _____
¿Qué? _____
¿Dónde? _____
¿Cuántos? _____
¿Cuánto? _____
¿Quién? _____
¿Cuándo? _____

> Without checking, can you give the meanings of these basic question words?

The following are *más* than just survival questions—they're *super!*

¿Le gusta?   Do you* like it?
¿Entiende?   Do you* understand?
¿Quisiera?   Would you (he, she) like some?
¿Hay?   Is there … *or* Are there any?
¿Por qué?   Why? (*Porque*, without the accent, is "Because")

¿Quiere?   Do you* want it?
¿Tiene?   Do you* have some?
¿Puede?   Can you (he, she) do it?

*Also: Does he *or* Does she.

¿Puede recordarlo? (Can You Remember It?)

Answer these questions with a Spanish word or phrase:

- ¿Cuál es su número de teléfono?
- ¿Cómo se dice "good-bye, yesterday, today, tomorrow, how, where"?
- ¿Dónde vive usted?
- ¿Cuántos años tiene usted?
- ¿Quién es su amigo y su amiga?

4

CHAPTER *CUATRO*

Mucho más

(Much More)

Do You Know Your ABC's? *(El alfabeto)*

¿Cómo se dice?

Once you get rolling, you'll find yourself asking people everywhere how to say things *en español.* At work, in public, or on the phone—learning words will simply be part of your everyday routine. Remember the following *preguntas?* Well, go ahead and use them to "pry."

> *¿Qué es esto?*   What's this?
> *¿Cómo se dice?*   How do you say it?
> *¿Qué significa?*   What does it mean?

They're *importantes,* yet sometimes you'll have to ask folks to "write it for you." Here are two lines that may help:

> *¿Cómo se escribe?*   How do you write it?
> *¿Cómo se deletrea?*   How do you spell it?

Simply hand them a pen and ask for it "*Letra por letra, por favor.*" ("Letter by letter, please.")

El alfabeto

First, the *easy* part:

1   You already know the Big Five—*a, e, i, o, u*—their names are just as they sound!

2   Well, these letters are "close" to English:

b	(beh "larga" or "grande")	*n*	('eh-neh)
v	(veh "corta" or "chica")	*p*	(peh)
c	(seh)	*q*	(coo)
d	(deh)	*r*	('eh-reh)
f	('eh-feh)	*s*	('eh-seh)
k	(kah)	*t*	(teh)
h	('ah-cheh)	*w*	(veh 'doh-bleh)
l	('eh-leh)	*x*	('eh-kees)
m	('eh-meh)		

3   And here we have the four Spanish letters most gringos have problems with:

g (heh)   *j* ('ho-tah)   *y* (ee-gree-'eh-gah)   *z* ('seh-tah)

4   The alfabeto also has **four more "letters"** than ours. Three of them are spelled with two letters together. And one has a ˜ on top!:

ch (cheh)   *ll* ('eh-yeh)   *rr* ('eh-rreh)   *ñ* ('en-yeh)

5   *Muy bien.* Are you ready to read the *alfabeto* in order? (Go somewhere "private" and *sing* it!)

a, b, c, ch, d, e, f, g, h, i, j, k, l, ll,
m, n, ñ, o, p, q, r, rr, s, t, u, v, w, x, y, z.

HOT TIPS!

- Spell *everything aloud* in Spanish from now on!
- But first, learn to spell your *nombre* and other *información de emergencia* (emergency information) just in case!
- Practice spelling over the *teléfono!*
- Use your *Diccionario* often! And practice looking up words ALOUD!
- Try teaching *inglés* words to a Spanish-speaking person. You'll be forced to spell!
- As you learned from the Secrets to Soundmaking, "close" is good enough!
- "ll" and "ch" have been cut from the official Spanish alphabet. However, people do refer to them when spelling out a word.

Take a *Número* (Number)

0   1   2   3   4   5   6   7   8   9

If you don't know these numbers, go back to *"¡Viva el vocabulario!"*

Sure, *los números* are easy. But do you realize how valuable they really are? In most cases, just by stating one number at a time, you can save yourself *muchos problemas!*

¿Cuál es su ...

What is your ...

Go ahead, answer the following "personal information," *número por número:*

número de teléfono   (phone number)? _____

_____

número de seguro social   (social security number)? _____

_____

número de licencia de chofer   (driver's license number)? _____

_____

domicilio or *dirección*   (address)? _____

código postal   (zip code)? _____

código de área   (area code)? _____

número del apartamento   (apartment number)? _____

número de placa   (license plate number)? _____

número de tarjeta de crédito   (credit card number)? _____

_____

número de facsímile   (fax number)? _____

número del celular   (cell phone number)? _____

You get the idea. Daily, practice saying aloud everything from your pocket change to the TV channels. *Remember* that the trick is to keep it fun!

Take Some More Numbers

Let's begin by breaking down *los números* just as we did the Spanish *alfabeto*—it helps the memory. Use your own word-association system, and stay motivated by thinking of new and exciting ways you can use to practice *every day!*

1 First, some *weird* numbers:

10	*diez*
11	*once*
20	*veinte*

> Practice these three until you can say them quickly and without *problemas!*

2 Next, the *easiest* ones:

12	*doce* (Hear the *"dos"*?)
13	*trece* (Hear the *"tres"*?)

3 Now, try to *picture these:*

14	*ca**tor**ce* (The number looks kind of "con**tor**ted")
15	*quince* (Pronounced "Kings say")

4 And how about some *math?*

(10) *diez y seis* (6) = (16) *dieciséis*
      diez y siete = (17) *diecisiete*
      diez y ocho = (18) *dieciocho*
      diez y nueve = (19) *diecinueve*

5 These multiples of *10* all end in—*nta*!:

Listen for the:

30	***tre**inta*	(***tre**s)*
40	***cua**renta*	(***cua**tro)*
50	***cincu**enta*	(***cinc**o)*
60	***ses**enta*	(***se**is)*
70	***set**enta*	(***siete**)*
80	***och**enta*	(***och**o)*
90	***nov**enta*	(***nuev**e)*

6 The numbers between are *all math problems!*:

(20) *veinte y uno* (1) = (21) *veintiuno*
____ *veinte y dos* ____ = (22) *veintidós*
____ *veinte y tres* ____ = (23) *veintitrés*
____ _____ ____ = ____

NOTE
In Spanish, check out the difference in the numerical form of the ordinals:
1st = 1ª or 1°
2nd = 2ª or 2°
3rd = 3ª or 3°
… and so on.

NOTE
Three more "toughies":
500 = *quinientos*
700 = *setecientos*
900 = *novecientos*
And guess what these are:
millón?   billón?

NOTE
Primero and *tercero* lose their final letter when placed in front of masculine singular words:
Mi primer carro.
My first car.
Está en el tercer grado.
He is in third grade.

7   100 is *cien* (like, "**cen**tury").
101 is *cien**to*** (+) *uno*.
201 is ***dos* cien*tos*** (+) *uno*.

8   1.000 is *mil* (like, "**mill**enium").
2.000 is *dos mil*, etc.
(Note that periods are used for thousands.)

9   **Order Up!**

1**st** *primera, – o*
2**nd** *segunda, – o*
3**rd** *tercera, – o*
4**th** *cuarta, – o*
5**th** *quinta, – o*
6**th** *sexta, – o*
7**th** *séptima, – o*
8**th** *octava, – o*
9**th** *novena, – o*
10**th** *décima, – o*

Instant Time Telling

Learning to tell someone what time it is in Spanish will take *no time* at all! Although there are other optional ways to do it, this is clearly the easiest and fastest way to go:

¿Qué hora es?
What time is it?

Listen for *"hora"* which means "the hour."

¿Qué horas son? means the same thing.

… To answer, just look at your **reloj** (a watch or clock!) and give the **hora** followed by the **minutos**.

6:15
seis y *quince*

> **NOTE**
> The *only change* is "half past." Then you say *y media* or *y treinta:* 6:30 = *seis y media.*
>
> To say, **"It's**–2:00 or more–use **Son las** … *dos, tres,* etc. (You don't say "o'clock.")
>
> *If it's 1:00–1:59 then use* **Es la** … *instead!*
>
> Try these: 7:45, 9:00, 1:30

OTHER "TIMELY TIDBITS"

… in the **morning**   *de la mañana*
… in the **afternoon**   *de la tarde*
… in the **evening**, at **night**   *de la noche*
Noon   *mediodía*
Midnight   *medianoche*

If you want to say "**At** (a certain time)," say **A las** …
at 6:15   "*a las seis y quince*"
Tiempo means "time, in general."
En punto means "on the dot."
Segundos are "seconds."

HOT TIPS!

- To tell time … notice you only need to know 1–59.
- Have others teach you some other ways to tell time!

International Date Line

Still another practical use of *los números* is the yearly calendar. Let's begin with the most common words and phrases having to do with *el calendario* (the calendar):

el día   the day
el mes   the month
la semana   the week
el año   the year

¡El calendario!

los días de la semana

el lunes	Monday
el martes	Tuesday
el miércoles	Wednesday
el jueves	Thursday
el viernes	Friday
el sábado	Saturday
el domingo	Sunday

los meses del año

1 enero	5 mayo	9 septiembre
2 febrero	6 junio	10 octubre
3 marzo	7 julio	11 noviembre
4 abril	8 agosto	12 diciembre

¿Cuál es la fecha?   What's the date?

The year is always read as one large number:

2010 = *dos mil diez*
(2000)   (10)

And whenever you give the date, apply the "Reversal Rule"!

June 3rd
el tres de junio

CHOOSE 'n USE!

Los días

Hay una fiesta …   There's a party … (on Saturday, on Friday, etc.)
¿Trabaja usted … ?   Do you work …? (on Monday, etc.)
El programa empieza …   The program begins … (on Thursday, etc.)

Los meses

Ayer fue el ___ de ___.   Yesterday was the (20th, etc.) of … (August, etc.)
Mi cumpleaños es en …   My birthday is in … (February, etc.)
¿Tiene usted las vacaciones en …?   Do you have vacation in …? (October, etc.)

Calendar Express!

Besides the basic calendar words it's nice to have other key words and expressions that will help get any date-line message across. As always, practice these *aloud* first, before you actually "go for it"!

The *"¿Qué día?"* questions:
- *¿Qué día es hoy?*   **What day** is today?
- *¿Qué día es mañana?*   **What day** is tomorrow?
- *¿Qué día fue ayer?*   **What day** was yesterday?
- *¿Qué día fue anteayer?*   **What day** was the day before yesterday?
- *¿Qué día es pasado mañana?*   **What day** is the day after tomorrow?

***¡Las estaciones!* (The Seasons!)**

la primavera   spring
el otoño   fall
el verano   summer
el invierno   winter

*¿Cuál es **su** estación favorita?* _____. (Which is **your** favorite season?)

¡Más palabras importantes en el calendario!

HOT TIP!

Hay ("there is" or "there are") is a *muy* useful calendar word! *Hay una fiesta mañana!*"

el próximo   the next one
el pasado   the past one
actual   current
ahora   now; nowadays

el aniversario   anniversary
la cita   appointment
diario   daily
la fiesta   party
el fin de semana   weekend
el horario   schedule
la reunión   meeting
las vacaciones   vacation

How's the Weather? (¿Qué tiempo hace?)

Making conversation with "weather chit-chat" is a *must* in any language and *¿Qué tiempo hace?* is a question that's *excelente* as an ice-breaker. Then, you're bound to need these:

Hace ...

It's

frío	cold
calor	hot
viento	windy
sol	sunny
buen tiempo	nice weather

Está ...

It's

despejado	clear
nublado	cloudy
nevando	snowing
lloviendo	raining
lloviznando	drizzling

Más Words:

el agua	water		*el huracán*	hurricane
el aire	air		*la luna*	moon
el cielo	sky		*la marea*	tide
las estrellas	stars		*los relámpagos*	lightning
el fuego	fire		*el terremoto*	earthquake
los grados	degrees		*la tormenta*	storm
el hielo	ice		*el trueno*	thunder
la inundación	flood		*el tornado*	tornado

NOTE

- Do not try to translate! Just think of **hace** as a "weather word," for now.
- *Calor* ("hot" for weather) *is not caliente* ("hot to the touch").

HOT TIPS!

- Here's the *easy way!*

  Hay ...
  There is
  or
  There are

neblina	fog
nubes	clouds
lluvia	rain
nieve	snow
humo	smoke

- If the *weather* is *not* moderate, use:

  ¡Hace mucho calor!
  It's very hot!
  ¡Hace mucho frío!
  It's very cold!
  nieva *mucho*
  It **snows** a lot
  llueve *mucho*
  It **rains** a lot

- *El clima* means "the climate."

¿*Puede recordarlo?*
(Can You Remember It?)

- Count to one hundred by tens in Spanish.
- Give your birthdate in Spanish.
- In Spanish, tell what the weather is like today.
- Translate into Spanish:
  What time is it?
  What's the date?
  What's this?
  What's your address?
  It's snowing.
- Translate into English:
  ¿Cuál es su código de área?
  Hay doce meses en un año.
  ¿Cuáles son los días de la semana?
  ¿Trabaja usted mañana?
  La siesta es hoy.

5

CHAPTER *CINCO*

Las personas

(People)

Es versus Está

Are you totally confused about the uses of **es** *and* **está?**

STOP THE FIGHT!
They're both right.

In Spanish, to say **is** or **you are**, it's **está** when referring to:
• **Location**   *¿Dónde está Carlos?—Él está allá!*
• **Condition**   *¿Cómo está Lupe?—Ella está muy bien.*
To indicate **"who"** or **"what"** is, use *es:*
Usted **es** *inteligente—Sí, pero, usted* **es** *más inteligente.*
María **es** *mexicana—No, ella* **es** *cubana.*

Notice the difference!
• *Está*
  Él **está** *bien.*   He **is** fine.
  La silla no **está** *en la sala.*   The chair **is** not in the living room.
  Ella **está** *trabajando.*   She **is** working.
• *Es*
  El programa **es** *importante.*   The program **is** important.
  María **es** *profesora.*   Maria **is** a professor.
  *¿***Es** *usted puertorriqueña?*   **Are** you Puerto Rican?
That's all you get for now! All this stuff is further explained in Chapter *Siete.*

Get It Together—Part I

It's time to begin linking your *palabras* together! Strings of words bound by logic create meaningful messages. And remembering that pronunciation and grammar have little effect on communication allows us to "babble away" more freely. Another helpful trick to recall is that words are joined in much the same order in Spanish as they are in *inglés!*

When we speak, *single words* and *one-liners* are the easiest ways to communicate our ideas:

> *¡Sí!*   Yes!
> *Él es.*   He is.

And adding words "to clarify" is *not* difficult:

> *¡Sí!, él es mi amigo.*   He is my friend.

Only, remember to use the "little linkers"—*y* (and), *o* (or), ***pero*** (but):

> *Él es mi amigo **y** ella es mi amiga, …*
> *… **¡pero** ella es más inteligente!*   … **but** she is more intelligent!

HOT TIPS!

- First, try *es* or *está*. Then, if your listener seems confused, smile and try it another way!
- In linking your Spanish words, recall and use these three concepts:
  1. The Reversal Rule
  2. The Once-and-for-all Rule
  3. The *El* and *La* Business
- Your Spanish pronunciation will improve the more you speak.

Do you remember any of this stuff?

El libro de José   Jose's book
es azul y rojo,   is blue and red,
pero está en su casa.   but it's at his house.
¿Cómo se llama?   What's your name?
¿Y dónde vive?   And where do you live?
En diciembre, hay nubes y hace mucho frío, y llueve mucho.
In December, it's cloudy and very cold, and it rains a lot.

Moreover, don't worry about "getting stuck." Just plug in an English word. (Although the last option may elicit a wince or a laugh from your listener.)

> *Él es mi amigo y ella es mi amiga, pero ella es más inteligente y más **rich!***

Un comentario about the *"tú"* form

Some readers might be wondering why I've only mentioned the "formal" *usted* form, and not the *tú* or so-called informal form of *es* and *está*. Think about it. *Why bother?* It just becomes another thing GRINGOS have to worry about. Spanish-speaking people use the intimate *tú* when speaking to their friends. But that's because they can understand each other! And they're bound by cultural ties. My point here is simple. By following these shortcuts, tips and Secrets to Success, *you too* will be able to make friends and establish "informal" relationships with Spanish-speaking people. Soon your new pals will be teaching you the *tú* form, along with lots of other "inside info." Besides, the *usted* form is easier to remember and use. You'll find it's perfectly acceptable when speaking with *anyone!*

"How Ya Doin'?"

We've talked already briefly about the question: *¿Cómo está usted?* (How are you?) We know that the answer, *Muy bien* (Very well), is the old stand-by! Now let's check out the many other responses that tell folks **how you feel**.

(*Estoy and soy* can be used without *yo!*)

If you want, try filling in the blanks:

Yo estoy _____.
Yo soy _____.
(**I** am ...)

fantástico(a)	fantastic	*sorprendido(a)*	surprised
bien	well	*cansado(a)*	tired
regular	OK	*orgulloso(a)*	proud
así-así	not bad	*débil*	weak
mal	not well	*fuerte*	strong
enfermo(a)	sick	*dormido(a)*	sleepy
feliz	happy	*aburrido(a)*	bored
triste	sad	*ansioso(a)*	anxious
ocupado(a)	busy	*enojado(a)*	angry
preocupado(a)	worried	*confundido(a)*	confused
nervioso(a)	nervous	*emocionado(a)*	excited

CHOOSE 'N USE!
- Estoy un poco ...   I'm a little ... (tired, sleepy, etc.).
- ¿Está usted muy ...?   Are you very ... (bored, anxious, etc.)?
- Carol está demasiado ... y ...   Carol is too ... (sad, etc.) and ... (worried).
- ¿Está ... usted?   Are you ... (surprised, etc.)?
- Es ... él?   Is he a ... (happy, excited, etc.) person?

HOT TIPS!

- With all the *palabras de descripción* (describing words), for emphasis, add:
  tan   so
  demasiado   too
  un poco   a little
  muy   very
- Put two or three of these adjectives with *y* (and)!
- *Remember:* **bueno** means "good," **bien** means "well."

NOTE

Es and *está* change what you're trying to say about a person's condition:
Él **está** *nervioso.*   He is nervous.
Él **es** *nervioso.*   He's a nervous person.

¡Qué cuerpo!
(What a Body!)

It's time to learn the Spanish names for different parts of the human body. After all, people are made *de carne y hueso* (of flesh and bone):

¡Ayyy! (Ouch!)

Here are some Spanish words and phrases to help you express what may go wrong with the body.

el accidente accident		***Dolor de ...***
la ambulancia ambulance		
la contusión bruise		*espalda* backache
la cortada cut		*muela* toothache
el dolor pain		*cabeza* headache
la emergencia emergency		*garganta* sore throat
la fiebre fever		*estómago* stomachache
la herida wound		
los primeros auxilios first aid		*Me duele.* It hurts.
la sangre blood		*Me siento mejor.* I feel better.
		Estoy malo(a). I'm ill.
		Estoy débil. I'm weak.
		Tengo resfriado. I have a cold.

Tengo resfriado en el pecho.   I have a cold in my chest.
Tengo fiebre.   I have a fever.
Me duele el estómago.   My stomach hurts.
¿Hay dolor en el cuello?   Is there a pain in the neck?
¿Hay cortadas en los brazos?   Are there cuts on the arms?
¡Llame al doctor!   Call the doctor!

Más partes del cuerpo:
la piel   skin
el corazón   heart
la lengua   tongue
el músculo   muscle
los pulmones   lungs

Family Ties

La gente and *las personas* both mean "the people."

Without a doubt, one of your initial encounters in Spanish will eventually lead to speaking about family members. But before we take a look at *la familia*, let's first make an effort to master these *muy importante* "people" *palabras:*

el hombre   man
la mujer   woman
el niño   small boy
la niña   small girl
el muchacho   young boy
la muchacha   young girl
el bebé   baby
el adolescente   teenager
el señor or *Sr.*   a man or Mr.
la señora or *Sra.*   a lady or Mrs.
la señorita or *Srta.*   a young unmarried woman
la persona   person
el socio   partner
el amigo   friend
el enemigo   enemy
los compañeros   buddies
los amantes   lovers
el novio   boyfriend or groom
la novia   girlfriend or bride
los novios   sweethearts or bride and groom
damas y caballeros   ladies and gentlemen
los parientes   relatives
los hijos   sons or sons and daughters
los hermanos   brothers or brother and sister
los papás or *padres*   parents
los abuelos   grandparents

HOT TIPS!

- Make the necessary changes for feminine and masculine, according to the *El* and *La* Business.
- To make more sentences, go ahead and insert words from both of the following categories.
  ¿Quién? words:
  yo, usted, ella, él, ellos nosotros, ustedes.
  ¡Posesión! words:
  mi, mis, su, sus, nuestro, nuestros.

Ella *es* **mi** *amiga.*

Más "Persona" Palabras!
cualquier persona   anyone
todo el mundo   everybody
poca gente   a few people
mucha gente   a lot of people

CHOOSE 'N USE!

- *Lupe es …*   Lupe is … (my little girl, my friend, etc.).
- *… está aquí.*   The … (man, baby, etc.) is here.
- *¿Quién es …?*   Who is the … (person, enemy, etc.)?
- *¿Son sus …?*   Are they your … (relatives, grandparents, etc.)?
- *Me gustan sus …*   I like your … (parents, brothers, etc.).
- *¿Dónde están …?*   Where are the … (lovers, sweethearts, etc.)?

NOTE

Los padrinos are "godparents"—in most Spanish-speaking countries, the in-laws and godparents are considered important family members! *Los compadres* is the name parents and godparents of a child share.

Los miembros de la familia
(The Family Members)

Touch these pictures with your finger. Read aloud, and check for meanings!

Él He   *Ella* She

Su   his, her, your, or their

Él es su esposo	*Ella es su esposa*
Él es su padre	*Ella es su madre*
Él es su hermano	*Ella es su hermana*
Él es su hijo	*Ella es su hija*
Él es su abuelo	*Ella es su abuela*

la sobrina	niece	*el sobrino*	nephew
el padre	father	*el yerno*	son-in-law
la madre	mother	*la nuera*	daughter-in-law
el abuelo	grandfather	*el cuñado*	brother-in-law
la abuela	grandmother	*la cuñada*	sister-in-law
el tío	uncle	*la hermana*	sister
la tía	aunt	*el hermano*	brother
el esposo or *el marido*	husband	*el hijo*	son
		la hija	daughter
la esposa	wife		
el suegro	father-in-law	*los nietos*	grandchildren
la suegra	mother-in-law	*los primos*	cousins

Familia **fine points:**

- The family unit is a vital part of Hispanic culture. Be sensitive.
- Other "terms of endearment" may be used besides the preceding words to name family members. Learn by asking or look them up in the dictionary if you need to.
- Notice how the informal *tú* is used for you instead of *usted* when family and friends talk to each other.
- Use *Es! Por ejemplo* (For example):

Es … He's or She's
mayor   older
menor   younger
un(a) gemelo(a)   a twin
casado(a)   married
soltero(a)   single

Él (Ella) *es …*
joven   young
viejo(a)   old
anciano(a)   very old

HOT TIP!

For affection, *-ita* and *-ito* can be added:
abuelita
hermanito
bebito

- Keep going:

la madrastra	stepmother
el padrastro	stepfather
la hijastra	stepdaughter
el hijastro	stepson

¿Puede recordarlo? (Can You Remember It?)

- Name three different emotions.
- Name three different body parts.
- Name three different family members.

¡*Mucho trabajo!*
(A Lot of Work!)

Most folks don't spend all of their time "hanging around" the relatives at home. They go to work. Let's expand our "people-talk" to include the words needed to chat about work. Notice how most of these words refer to males only:

Los trabajadores (The workers)

el abogado	lawyer	*el enfermero*	nurse
el arquitecto	architect	*el estudiante*	student
el asistente	assistant	*el gerente*	manager
el bombero	firefighter	*el ingeniero*	engineer
el cajero	cashier	*el jardinero*	gardener
el camarero or *mesero*	waiter	*el jefe*	boss
el camionero	truck driver	*el maestro*	teacher
el campesino	farmer	*el mecánico*	mechanic
el carpintero	carpenter	*el músico*	musician
el cliente	client	*el pintor*	painter
el cocinero	chef	*el plomero*	plumber
el criado	servant	*el policía*	police officer
el dentista	dentist	*el secretario*	secretary
el dependiente	clerk	*el soldado*	soldier
el doctor	doctor	*el obrero*	factory worker
el dueño	owner	*el vendedor*	salesman
el empleado	employee	*el técnico*	technician
el empresario	employer	*el ayudante*	helper
		el chofer	driver

Some rather unique *profesiones:*

el payaso clown
el astronauta astronaut
la actriz actress

el atleta athlete
el ladrón thief
el escritor writer

CHOOSE 'N USE!
- *¿Quién es ...?* Who is the ... (boss, chef, teacher, etc.)?
- *Quiere ser ...* He/She wants to be a ... (writer, farmer, lawyer, etc.).
- *... es excelente.* The ... (painter, mechanic, actress, etc.) is excellent.

HOT TIPS!

- *¿Qué hace?* means "What do you do?" (also, What does *he* or *she* do?)
- Make sentences! Just put **Es** in front! (**Es** = he's, she's, you're.)
- *Sí,* these words **do** require the *El* and *La* Business, based on the worker's gender.

Trabajo, trabajo, trabajo …

There's really no way to present all the Spanish words related to *el trabajo* because we all hold different *trabajos*. The following is a *colección* of miscellaneous stuff. If you need to know the name of something specific at your workplace, ask a Spanish speaker for some help. (Remember: **¿Qué es esto en español?** is "What is this thing called in Spanish?")

Work on these words:

la agencia	agency	*el horario*	schedule
el almacén	warehouse	*la huelga*	strike
el cheque	check	*la junta*	meeting
la cita	appointment	*la lista*	list
la computadora	computer	*la máquina*	machine
la conferencia	conference	*el archivo*	file
el contrato	contract	*el material*	material
la copiadora	copier	*la oficina*	office
el correo	mail	*el producto*	product
el entrenamiento	training	*el programa*	program
la entrevista	interview	*la reparación*	repair
la fábrica	factory	*la tarjeta*	time card
los formularios	forms	*la venta*	sale
la herramienta	tool	*la impresora*	printer

CHOOSE 'N USE!

- *¿Dónde está …?* Where's the … (factory, meeting, etc.)?
- *Hay problemas con …* There are problems with the … (tool, machine, etc.).
- *Me gusta …* I like the … (program, schedule, etc.).
- *Necesito mi …* I need my … (check, contract, etc.).

The Good, the Bad, and the Ugly

Describing people in Spanish is no different from describing places and things. As you've discovered you can rely on the Reversal Rule! Whenever you want to add a *description*, simply think *backwards*.

*Él es un **hombre grande**.*

He is a **big man.**

NOTE
A different way to say the same thing is—*El hombre es grande.* And of course you'll need the *El* and *La* Business and the Once-and-for-All Rule:
Ellas son señoritas bonitas. They are pretty girls.

HOT TIPS!

- These words can be easily remembered through "word-picture association"!
- "Describing" in Spanish seems *strange* at first, but soon, the "GRINGO" brain will make the switch automatically!
- Some *descripciones do not change* because they don't end in **a** or **o**: *Un hombre grande. Una señorita grande.*
- Some words change a little and go immediately in front of the noun. *Él es **un buen** amigo.* He's a very good friend. *Ella es una **gran** persona.* She's a great person. *Ella está **mal** preparada.* She is poorly prepared.
- Did you know that *los colores* are *descripción* words? *El radio es grande y negro.* The radio is big and black.

Now, why not delve into these describers!

grande big	*feo(a)* ugly	*simpático(a)* nice
chico(a) small	*bonito(a)* pretty	*extraño(a)* strange
bueno(a) good	*guapo(a)* handsome	*fuerte* strong
malo(a) bad		*débil* weak
nuevo(a) new	*alto(a)* tall	*largo(a)* long
viejo(a) old	*flaco(a)* thin	*bajo(a)* short in height
joven young	*gordo(a)* fat	*corto(a)* short in length
perezoso(a) lazy		
trabajador(a) industrious		

HOT TIPS!

- *Descripción* words that start with *in-* usually refer to an opposite: *correcto* ‣ *incorrecto* (not correct).
- There are countless *descripciones* which are easy to recall because *they're a lot like English:* *favorito* *natural* *sincero* *moderno* *popular* *elegante* *terrible* *furioso* *Be on the lookout* for "fakers." *Embarazada*, for example, does not mean "embarrassed"—it means pregnant!
- Now that you are putting two or more words together *on your own*, here's a suggestion: Be proud of yourself! Self-confidence builds from little successes. So whenever you describe—*relax* and just ramble on!
- For a complete *descripción*, do so as you would in *inglés.* The house is **big, red,** and **green.** *La casa es* **grande, roja y verde.**

Use these "little words" to elaborate:

más grande.   bigger
lo más grande.   biggest
tan grande cómo ...
    as big as ...

Él es — He's
- *un poco*   a little
- *muy*   very
- *demasiado*   too
- *tan*   so

— *lento.* slow.

Más Descripciones!

tonto(a)	dumb	*moreno(a)*	dark-haired
inteligente	smart	*pelirrojo(a)*	red-headed
brillante	bright	*calvo(a)*	bald
sucio(a)	dirty	*duro(a)*	hard
limpio(a)	clean	*blando(a)*	soft
lento(a)	slow	*rico(a)*	rich
rápido(a)	fast	*pobre*	poor
vacío(a)	empty	*valiente*	brave
lleno(a)	full	*cobarde*	cowardly
claro(a)	light	*interesante*	interesting
oscuro(a)	dark	*peligroso(a)*	dangerous
mayor	older	*roto(a)*	broken
menor	younger	*ancho(a)*	wide
fácil	easy	*estrecho(a)*	narrow
difícil	difficult	*suave*	smooth
barato(a)	inexpensive	*áspero(a)*	rough
caro(a)	expensive	*famoso(a)*	famous
frío(a)	cold	*equivocado(a)*	wrong
caliente	hot to touch	*disponible*	available
picante	hot to taste	*maravilloso(a)*	marvelous
rubio(a)	blond	*perdido(a)*	lost

CHOOSE 'N USE!

- *Marco no es ...*   Marco isn't ... (rich, bald, young, etc.).
- *Mi carro parece ...*   My car seems ... (full, slow, dirty, etc.).
- *Quiero algo ...*   I want something ... (dark, soft, etc.).
- *Usted no es muy ...*   You aren't very ... (fat, old, etc.).
- *Él es ..., ..., y ...*   He's ... (handsome, etc.), ..., (tall, etc.), and ... (nice).
- *¿Kim es ... o ...?*   Is Kim ... (lazy, etc.) or ... (industrious)?

6

CHAPTER *SEIS*

Las cosas

(Things)

"Mi casa es su casa"

As with all new words, it's best to learn these through "experience." Have a friend or another person command you to *move, point, pick up, carry,* or just *touch* the following common household objects:

Mueva ...
Move ...

Señale ...
Point to ...

Recoja ...
Pick up ...

Toque ...
Touch ...

Mire ...
Look at ...

Limpie ...
Clean ...

el sofá

el sillón

la lámpara

la silla

el televisor

el estéreo

las pinturas

la mesa

la puerta

el teléfono

la tina

el librero

la chimenea

la cama

la estufa

el refrigerador

el excusado

el lavabo

el reloj

el tocador

CHOOSE 'N USE!
- … *está quebrado(a).*   The … (lamp, refrigerator, etc.) is broken.
- *No puedo encontrar …*   I can't find the … (table, chair, etc.).
- *¿Cuánto cuesta …?*   How much is the … (computer, stove, etc.)?

¡Más cosas en la casa!

la alfombra   rug
la aspiradora   vacuum cleaner
los cajones   drawers
el cesto de basura   trash can
las cortinas   curtains
los gabinetes   cabinets
la lavadora   washer
la licuadora   blender
el ropero   closet
la secadora   dryer
el tostador   toaster
el trapeador   mop
los trastes   dishes
los cubiertos   silverware

¡Más aún (More still)

la almohada   pillow
el balde   bucket
la cobija   blanket
la escoba   broom
el espejo   mirror
el jabón   soap
la plancha   iron
la ducha   shower
la sábana   sheet
la toalla   towel
la esponja   sponge

CHOOSE 'N USE!
- *No tiene un/una …*   It doesn't have a … (cabinet, closet, etc.).
- *No me gusta el color de …*   I don't like the color of the … (rugs, curtains, etc.).

HOT TIP!

Lots of household objects can be said in English and are easier if left untranslated! (Discover more on your own!)

el switch
el microwave
los CD's
los speakers
el laptop

¿Dónde está?

Next time you can't find what you're looking for around *la casa*, send out a search party *en español!*

Here are a few places where it's most likely to be found.

Está en …
It's in (on, *or* at) the …

el dormitorio bedroom	*el baño* bathroom
las escaleras stairs	*el césped* grass, lawn
el sótano basement	*la cocina* kitchen
el pasillo hallway	*el jardín* garden
la sala living room	*el garaje* garage
el comedor dining room	*el piso* floor
el techo roof	*el cuarto* room
el desván attic	*el apartamento* apartment

Vocabulario especial

Voy a comprar …
I'm going to buy …

No tengo …
I don't have …

¿Puede Ud. reparar …?
Can you repair …?

el aire acondicionado   air conditioning
las llaves   keys
la electricidad   electricity
los muebles   furniture
los enchufes   outlets
el portón   gate
la calefacción   heating
las cerraduras   locks
la tubería   plumbing
las luces   lights
la cerca   fence
el timbre   doorbell
las repisas   shelves

CHOOSE 'N USE!
- *Voy a buscar ...*   I'm going to look for ... (furniture, locks etc.).
- *No tengo un/una ...*   I don't have a ... (basement, attic, etc.).
- *¿Puede reparar ...?*   Can you repair ... (the plumbing, stairs, etc.)?

Las herramientas (Tools)
los alicates   pliers
el clavo   nail
el destornillador   screwdriver
la escalera   ladder
la manguera   hose
el martillo   hammer
la pala   shovel
el rastrillo   rake
el serrucho   saw
las tijeras   scissors
el tornillo   screw
la pintura   paint
la cinta   tape
la llave inglesa   wrench

Los materiales (Materials)
el alambre   wire
el asfalto   asphalt
la baldosa   floor tile
el cartón   cardboard
el cemento   cement
la goma   rubber
el ladrillo   brick
la madera   wood
la piedra   stone
el plástico   plastic
la tela   cloth

HOT TIP!

Try these wonderful one-liners.
Se me perdió.   I lost it.
Se me olvidó.   I forgot it.
Se me quebró.   I broke it.

La vida en la ciudad grande
(Life in the big city)

Spanish fills our cities, ... so let's leave the comfy confines of **la casa** and head into town. Walk, ride, or drive around *pointing* and *naming* things. (If you're caught talking to yourself, *don't stop!* It'll be too hard to explain.)

Los edificios (Buildings)
el almacén   warehouse, store
el banco   bank
la biblioteca   library
el cine   movie theater
el correo   post office
el departamento de bomberos
  fire department
la escuela   school
la estación de policía   police
  station
la fábrica   factory
la farmacia   pharmacy
la gasolinera   gas station
el hospital   hospital
la iglesia   church
el museo   museum
la oficina   office
el restaurante   restaurant
el supermercado   supermarket
la tienda   store

Los lugares y sitios
(Places and sites)
el aeropuerto   airport
la acera   sidewalk
el barrio or *el*
  vecindario   neighborhood
la calle   street
el camino   road
la carretera   highway
el centro   downtown
la cuadra   city block
el ascensor   elevator
la esquina   corner
el metro   subway
el parque   park
el pueblo   town
el puente   bridge
el estacionamiento   parking lot

Keep looking around:
el semáforo   traffic light
el buzón   mailbox
la parada de   bus stop
  autobús

CHOOSE 'N USE!

- *¿Sabe dónde está …?*   Do you know where the … (museum, bank, etc.) is?
- *… está cerca de …*   The … (church, etc.) is near the … (school, etc.).
- *Espéreme Ud. en …*   Wait for me at the … (subway, corner, etc.).

La transportación
(Transportation)

el carro or *el coche* or *el automóvil*

el helicóptero

la bicicleta

el camión

el barco

el avión

el autobús

el tren (train)
el metro (subway)

la motocicleta

el taxi

CHOOSE 'N USE!

- *¿Va por … o …?*   Are you going by … (taxi, etc.) or … (train, etc.)?
- *No me gusta viajar por …*   I don't like traveling by … (airplane, etc.).
- *Busco …*   I'm looking for the … (bus, etc.).

Más City Life

la piscina   pool
el rascacielos   skyscraper
el cementerio   cemetery
la cárcel   jail
la cantina   bar
las afueras   outskirts
el lote de carros   car lot
el zoológico   zoo
el campamento   campgrounds

There is a little piece of language—*ería*—(pronounced air-EE-ah) that is found *at the end* of words which name *stores* and *shops*. Watch the pattern!

la tortillería   tortilla factory
la mueblería   furniture store
la zapatería   shoe store
la carnicería   meat market
la joyería   jewelry store
la panadería   bakery
la peluquería   barber shop

As you travelers can see, the **ería** ending will work wonders for you as you're finding your way around *la ciudad grande.*

HOT TIPS!

• You may need these:
Las direcciones
N *(Norte)*
O *(Oeste)*
E *(Este)*
S *(Sur)*
• And fill out that form:
el condado
(county) _____
el estado
(state) _____
el país
(country) _____

Unas naciones y nacionalidades

Meeting people from many different parts of the world is becoming increasingly common. Here are some words to give your Spanish conversation an international flair.

España Spain	*español(-ola)* Spanish
México Mexico	*mexicano(a)* Mexican
Francia France	*francés(-esa)* French
Cuba Cuba	*cubano(a)* Cuban
Los Estados Unidos United States (EEUU = USA)	*americano(a)* American
Puerto Rico Puerto Rico	*puertorriqueño(a)* Puerto Rican
Inglaterra England	*inglés(-esa)* English
Irlanda Ireland	*irlandés(-esa)* Irish
Japón Japan	*japonés(-esa)* Japanese
China China	*chino(a)* Chinese
Alemania Germany	*alemán(ana)* German
Italia Italy	*italiano(a)* Italian
Canadá Canada	*canadiense* Canadian

- *Centroamérica* Central America
- *Norteamérica* North America
- *Sudamérica* South America
- *Europa* Europe
- *Oriente Medio* Middle East
- *África* Africa

¡Razas!

Asiático Asian
Blanco White
Negro o afroamericano Black or African American
Indio o amerindio Native American
Hispano Hispanic

CHOOSE 'N USE!
- *Me voy a mudar a ___.* I'm moving to …
- *Está en la frontera de ___.* It's on the border of …
- *¿Ha ido a___?* Have you been to …

HOT TIPS!
- Unlike in English, nationalities are *not* capitalized!
- *La frontera* is "the border."
- *¿Adónde va Ud.?* Where are you going?
- *¡Voy a hacer un viaje!* I'm taking a trip!

Back to Nature

Let's get out of town for a while! But before we take off, why don't we "handle" a few of nature's little wonders that are within "reach"—right outside the door! And as we do with all new words of objects—let's *touch 'n talk*.

La naturaleza
(Nature)

el árbol	tree
el arbusto	bush
la arena	sand
la flor	flower
el pasto	grass
la hoja	leaf
el lodo	mud
el palo	stick
la piedra	rock
la planta	plant
el polvo	dust
la rama	branch
la semilla	seed
la tierra	dirt

Los insectos
(Insects)

la abeja	bee
la araña	spider
la hormiga	ant
la mosca	fly
el grillo	cricket
la avispa	wasp
el zancudo	mosquito
la cucaracha	beetle

Los animales
(Animals)

Los domésticos
(the "domestic ones")
el caballo horse
el chivo goat
el gato cat
la oveja sheep
el pájaro bird
el pato duck
el perro dog
el pez fish
el pollo chicken
el puerco pig
el ratón mouse
la vaca cow
la tortuga turtle
el conejo rabbit

Sometimes, animals aren't so easy to "handle," but have fun anyway!

Los salvajes
(the "wild ones"):
el camello camel
la cebra zebra
el elefante elephant
el hipopótamo
   hippopotamus
la jirafa giraffe
el león lion
el mono monkey
el oso bear
el rinoceronte
   rhinoceros
el tigre tiger
el venado deer
la víbora snake
el lobo wolf
el águila eagle

CHOOSE 'N USE!

- *Hay … allí.*   There's … (a flower, a goat, etc.) over there.
- *¿Tiene …?*   Does it have … (bushes, chickens, etc.)?
- *No me gusta …*   I don't like … (mud, spiders, etc.).
- *¿Ha visto …?*   Have you seen the … (rock, camel, etc.)?
- *… es mi favorito.*   The … (tiger, tree, etc.) is my favorite.
- *… no es peligroso(a).*   The … (zebra, etc.) isn't dangerous.
- *… come mucho.*   The … (bear, lion, etc.) eats a lot.
- *… es inteligente.*   The … (monkey, dog, etc.) is smart.
- *… vive en la selva.*   The … (hippopotamus, etc.) lives in the jungle.

Now let our words head for

el campo
(the countryside):

el bosque   forest
el cerro   hill
la costa   coast
el desierto   desert
el lago   lake
el mar   sea
la montaña   mountain
la playa   beach
el arroyo   stream

el rancho   ranch
el río   river
la selva   jungle
el valle   valley
la cueva   cave
la finca   farm

CHOOSE 'N USE!

- *… es maravilloso(a).*   The … (ranch, coast, etc.) is marvelous.
- *Ellos viven en …*   They live in the … (valley, ocean, etc.).
- *¡Vamos a …!*   Let's go to the … (lake, desert, etc.)!

"I'm Hungry" *(Tengo hambre)*

Food words, too, may differ slightly from *región* to *región*, but don't get nervous; instead, eat and ask! The words that follow can be used safely everywhere!

La comida
(Food!)

el bistec steak	*el jamón* ham
el camarón shrimp	*la langosta* lobster
el cangrejo crab	*la mantequilla* butter
la carne meat	*la nuez* nut
el cereal cereal	*el pan* bread
el cerdo pork	*el pastel* pie
el dulce candy	*el pavo* turkey
la ensalada salad	*el perro caliente* hot dog
la galleta cookie	*el pescado* fish
la goma de mascar	*el pollo* chicken
or *el chicle* gum	*el queso* cheese
la hamburguesa burger	*la salchicha* sausage
el helado ice cream	*la sopa* soup
el huevo egg	*la torta* cake
el arroz rice	*el fideo* noodle

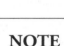

> **NOTE**
> Try to "mumble" these words before you *dig in!*

Las frutas
(Fruit)

la cereza cherry	*la naranja* orange	*el melocotón* peach
la fresa strawberry	*el plátano* banana	*le pera* pear
el limón lemon	*la toronja* grapefruit	*la piña* pineapple
la manzana apple	*la uva* grape	*el coco* coconut

Los vegetales
(Vegetables)

la cebolla onion	*el tomate* tomato	*la zanahoria* carrot
la col or *el repollo*	*la lechuga* lettuce	*los frijoles* beans
cabbage	*el maíz* corn	*el apio* celery
el guisante or *chícharo*	*la patata* or	*la espinaca* spinach
pea	*papa* potato	*el pepino* cucumber

La cocina
(Kitchen)

la cafetera	coffee pot	*la olla*	pot	*el delantal*	apron
el sartén	frying pan	*la receta*	recipe	*el mantel*	tablecloth

CHOOSE 'N USE!

- *La ensalada tiene …*   The salad has … (carrots, onions, etc.).
- *¡ … es dulce!*   The … (corn, orange, etc.) is sweet!
- *No puedo comer …*   I can't eat … (lemons, strawberries, etc.).
- *¿Quisiera una … o …?*   Would you like a … (banana, etc.) or a … (grapefruit)?
- *… huele mal.*   The … (lettuce, etc.) smells bad.
- *¿Quiere …?*   Do you want a … (tablecloth, etc.)?
- *Voy a comprar …*   I'm going to buy a … (vase, etc.).

"Restaurante" Remarks

¡Qué …
How
deliciosa (or *sabrosa*)!
   delicious!
picante!   hot (to taste)!
caliente!   hot (to touch)!

Quisiera (I'd like) …
or
Ella tiene (She has) …
or
Tráigame (Bring me) …

algo de comer.   something to eat.
algo de beber.   something to drink.
el plato del día.   today's special.
el menú.   a menu.
más agua.   more water.
la cuenta.   the bill.
el postre.   the dessert.

¿Está …
Is it …
crudo(a)?   raw?
cocido(a)?   cooked?
frito(a)?   fried?
fresco(a)?   fresh?
maduro(a)?   ripe?
podrido(a)?   rotten?

Now munch on these helpful tidbits:
Estoy en dieta.   I'm on a diet.
Para comer aquí.   To eat here.
Para llevar.   To go.
Quiero ordenar.   I want to order.
las comidas   The meals
el desayuno   breakfast
el almuerzo   lunch
la cena   dinner

Eat using these words:
la botella   bottle
la camarera or *mesera*   waitress
el camarero or *mesero*   waiter
el (la) cocinero(a)   cook
la cuchara   spoon
el cuchillo   knife
el platillo   saucer
el plato   plate
el pimentero   pepper shaker
la servilleta   napkin
la taza   cup
el tenedor   fork
el salero   salt shaker
el vaso   glass

Tengo sed
(I'm thirsty)
el batido   milk shake
la bebida   a drink
el café   coffee
el café descafeinado
    decaffeinated coffee
la cerveza   beer
el hielo   ice
el jugo   juice
la leche   milk
la limonada   lemonade
el refresco   soft drink
el té   tea
el vino   wine

Los sabores   *Los ingredientes*
(Flavors)   (Ingredients)

Está ...	*el aceite* oil	*la harina* flour
It's ...	*el ajo* garlic	*la miel* honey
dulce. sweet.	*la canela* cinnamon	*la mostaza* mustard
amargo(a). bitter.	*el azúcar* sugar	*la pimienta* pepper
agrio(a). sour.	*el condimento* spice	*la sal* salt
seco(a). dry.	*la crema* cream	*la salsa* sauce
salado(a). salty.	*el vinagre* vinegar	*la vainilla* vanilla

CHOOSE 'N USE!
- *Necesito ...*   I need the ... (waiter, napkin, etc.).
- *... está sucio(a).*   The ... (glass, fork, etc.) is dirty.
- *Se me cayó ...*   I dropped the ... (spoon, cup, etc.).
- *Necesita más ...*   It needs more ... (sauce, mustard, etc.).
- *Hay demasiado(a) ...*   There's too much ... (salt, garlic, etc.).
- *No bebo ...*   I don't drink ... (wine, juice, etc.).
- *¿Quiere Ud. ... o ...?*   Do you want ... (coffee) or ... (tea)?
- *... está horrible.*   The ... (drink, etc.) is horrible.

HOT TIP!

Use *mucho* and *poco* for a **large** and **small** "amount." *Muchos* and *pocos* are for **many** and **a few**!

"What Are You Wearing?" (¿Qué lleva?)

… Get dressed in Spanish! The next time you're putting something on, name it *en español!*

NOTES
La ropa
(Clothing)
… *para* **mujeres**
   women's
… *para* **hombres**   men's
… *para* **niños**   children's

Clothing Commands!
- Take off your clothes!
  (*¡Quítese la ropa!*)
- Get dressed! (*¡Vístase!*)
- Put it on! (*¡Póngaselo!*)

el abrigo   overcoat
la bata de baño   bathrobe
la blusa   blouse
las botas   boots
las bragas   panties
la bufanda   scarf
los calcetines   socks
los calzoncillos   shorts
la camisa   shirt
la camiseta   T-shirt
la chaqueta   jacket
el cinturón   belt
la corbata   tie
la falda   skirt
la gorra   cap
los guantes   gloves
el impermeable   raincoat
las medias   stockings
los pantalones   pants
el pijama   pajamas
la ropa interior
   underwear
el saco   sportscoat
el sombrero   hat
las sudaderas   sweatsuit
el suéter   sweater
los tenis   tennis shoes
el traje   suit
el traje de baño   bathing
   suit
el vestido   dress
las zapatillas   slippers
los zapatos   shoes

Más cosas importantes:
el botón   button
el bolsillo   pocket
el cierre   zipper

CHOOSE 'N USE!
- *¿Dónde compró Ud. …?*
  Where did you buy the … (jacket, shirt, etc.)?
- *Me gusta el color de …*
  I like the color of the … (blouse, pants, etc.).
- *Necesito …*   I need the … (slippers, suit, etc.).
- *¿Cuánto cuesta …?*   How much is the … (dress, overcoat, etc.)?
- *… son muy viejos(as).*   The … (shoes, shorts, etc.) are very old.

Lavar la ropa
(Washing clothes)

"The cleaners" are *la lavandería*
"Dirty laundry" is *la ropa sucia*
"Detergent" is *el detergente*
"Stain" is *la mancha*
"Bleach" is *el blanqueador*
"Hangers" are *los ganchos*

HOT TIPS!
- Describe clothes with *los colores!*
- *Un par de* is "a pair of"
- You may hear *different words* used to name these things. *Who cares?* These will work fine!

¿Puede recordarlo? (Can You Remember It?)

In Spanish:
- Name three job titles.
- Name three descriptive words.
- Name three pieces of furniture.
- Name three rooms in the house.
- Name three buildings in the city.
- Name three plants or animals.
- Name three foods or beverages.
- Name three articles of clothing.

"Let's Go Shopping"
(¡Vamos de compras!)

el dinero   money
el cheque   check
la tarjeta de crédito
   credit card

el cambio   change
la cuenta   bill
el cupón   coupon
el descuento   discount
el enganche   down payment
la ganga   bargain
la oferta   offer
el pago   payment
el precio   price
el recibo   receipt
la venta   sale

La joyería
(Jewelry Store)

el anillo   ring
los aretes   earrings
el brazalete   bracelet
el broche   brooch
la cadena   chain
el collar   necklace

los diamantes   diamonds
las joyas   jewels
el oro   gold
las perlas   pearls
la plata   silver
el reloj   watch

Buyer's Babble!

¿Es todo? Is that all?

¡Me gusta! I like it!

¿Qué marca es? What brand is it?

No me queda bien. It doesn't fit.

Me quedo con esto. I'll take this.

¿Cuánto cuesta? (or *¿Cuánto vale?)* How much is it?

¿Cuánto pesa? How much does it weigh?

Quiero probármelo. I want to try it on.

Quiero cargarlo a mi cuenta. I want to charge it (to my account).

¿En qué puedo servirle? Can I help you?

¿Algo más? Something else?

¿Cuánto por ciento? What percent?

Es gratis. It's free.

Necesito un dependiente. I need a clerk.

Quiero un(a) cajero(a). I want a cashier.

¿Cuál departamento? Which department?

Unas Extras

la bolsa bag; purse

la caja box

la cartera wallet

el cepillo brush

la cinta ribbon

la maleta suitcase

el maletín briefcase

el maquillaje make-up

la mochila knapsack

el paraguas umbrella

el peine comb

el perfume perfume

el espejo mirror

la canasta basket

¿Cuál es su talla?

(What's your size?)

Uso un ...

I take a ...

chico small

mediano medium

grande large

extra X large

CHOOSE 'N USE!

- *Busco ...* I am looking for the ... (sale, perfume, etc.).
- *Quisiera ...* I'd like the ... (receipt, change, etc.).
- *¿Se vende ...?* Do you sell ... (rings, combs, etc.)?
- *¿Dónde están ...?* Where are the ... (suitcases, diamonds, etc.)?

"Get into the Act!"

There's no better way to learn than by *doing*. That is why the best language programs include *commands* as a method to teach both *actions* as well as *objects*.

¡Cante la canción!
Sing the song!
¡Salude la bandera!
Salute the flag!

Commands involve both the speaker and the listener.

With friends and family, take turns giving each other *mandatos* (commands). Select common objects, and using the commands below, act them out! (They're great for work or play!)

Mueva (Move)   **la**
Lleve (Carry)   **televisión**
Levante (Raise)   (television)
Prenda (Turn on)   or
Traiga (Bring)   **esto**
Toque (Touch)   (this)
Señale (Point to)   or
Baje (Lower)   **eso**
Apague (Turn off)   (that)
Mire (Watch)

¡Más mandatos!

Baile	Dance	*Firme*	Sign	*Regrese*	Return
Busque	Look for	*Lave*	Wash	*Repita*	Repeat
Cante	Sing	*Lea*	Read	*Saque*	Take out
Coma	Eat	*Limpie*	Clean	*Siga*	Continue
Compre	Buy	*Llame*	Call	*Suba*	Climb
Conteste	Answer	*Mande*	Send	*Tire*	Throw
Corra	Run	*Marque*	Dial	*Tome*	Drink
Escriba	Write	*Meta*	Put inside	*Vea*	See
Escuche	Listen	*Pida*	Ask for	*Venda*	Sell
Estudie	Study	*Quite*	Take away	*Venga*	Come

Let's make a *mandato!*

A simple approach to forming a command in Spanish requires knowledge of the three different action word (verb) endings. The endings are:

> *ar* as in *hablar*   to speak
> *er* as in *comer*   to eat
> *ir* as in *escribir*   to write

To make a *mandato*, drop the last two letters of the infinitive ("to") form and replace them as follows:

> *ar* → *e*
> *hablar* → *¡Hable!*   Speak!
>
> *er* → *a*
> *comer* → *¡Coma!*   Eat!
>
> *ir* → *a*
> *escribir* → *¡Escriba!*   Write!

But **beware**! Some verbs are weird and simply have to be memorized.

> *ir* → *¡Vaya!*   Go!
> *venir* → *¡Venga!*   Come!
> *decir* → *¡Diga!*   Speak!

HOT TIPS!

- Because commands are exchanged so often between friends, you may hear folks using the *tú* (or informal) form of the action words. Don't get excited. Here are a few common "informal" commands:
  ¡Ven!   Come here!
  ¡Vete!   Go away!
  ¡Dime!   Tell me!
  ¡Espérate!   Wait!
  ¡Cállate!   Shut up!
  ¡Llámame!   Call me!
- Use the previously listed commands for now, and don't worry about forming your own yet. You'll get the idea with practice!
- To tell someone *not* to do something, just put **no** in front of the command!
- When you can't remember the name of an object, use **esto** for "this thing" or **eso** for "that thing."
- You can always get your idea across by simply using the basic action (verb) form preceded by *favor de* (please).
  Favor de hablar.
  Please speak.
  Favor de seguir.
  Please continue.
- Start now by following these simple commands!
  ¡Toque el libro!
  Touch the book!
  ¡Escriba su nombre!
  Write your name!
  ¡Baile la salsa!
  Dance the *salsa!*

Los Mighty *Mandatos!*

Here are some common commands that are almost always given alone, and they work well *all by themselves!* (They are actually two words rolled into one.)

¡Acuéstese!	Lie down!
¡Agárrelo!	Grab it!
¡Cálmese!	Calm down!
¡Créame!	Believe me!
¡Cúidese!	Take care of yourself!
¡Déjelo!	Leave it alone!
¡Démelo!	Give it to me!
¡Despiértese!	Wake up!

¡Dígame!	Tell me!
¡Espérese!	Wait!
¡Hágalo!	Do it!
¡Levántese!	Stand up!
¡Párese!	Stop!
¡Pregúntele!	Ask him or her!
¡Recójalo!	Pick it up!
¡Siéntese!	Sit down!
¡Vamos!	Let's go!

As you speak, help convey meaning through facial expressions and body language.

7

CHAPTER *SIETE*

¡Acción!

(Action!)

Un Anuncio Importante

You are about to enter the next level of proficiency in Spanish.

Please read:

• This chapter introduces Spanish action words or verbs. Do not be afraid! There is no "conjugating." Instead, general suggestions are made, and *practical* action word lists are presented here. But you still have to pay attention. Believe it or not, this stuff is what *makes Spanish really work!*

• As always, *mistakes are good*, so don't hold back. Keep a positive attitude, and do the best you can. Don't worry about every word! Use only what you need.

NOTE
Spanish is easy! Most *action words have the same base form.* This means that all you have to do to understand action words is focus on the *first part* of the word. Here's how it works: First, take a typical action, like "to work" (*trabajar*). Now let's see what the base **trabaj-** can do!
¡Trabaj-en! (Work!)
¡Trabaj-aron! (They worked!)
¡Trabaj-amos! (We work!)
¡Trabaj-ando! (Working!)
¡Trabaj-aba! (I used to work!)
¡Trabaj-aría! (I would work!)

Basics in Action

There are only three action word endings. The basic word-forms end in *-ar, -er* or *-ir*. That's it. Action words can be used all by themselves. You won't always be correct, but people will still understand. To get "extensive training" in *action words* (verbs), buy a textbook, or take a class. But for simple communication, try to pick up on the vocabulary and tips that follow.

A Big Step Toward Fluency

Words and one-liners are great, if you like to keep things short. But to make a Spanish conversation last, sooner or later you'll need the "to be" words, *estar* and *ser* (**"The Big 8"**).

Remember: you can drop the *quién* words if you like.

Estar

It seems GRINGOS tend to pick up the following words right away:

Yo	**estoy**	I **am**
Usted *Él* *Ella* *(Una cosa)*	**está**	You **are** He **is** She **is** It **is**
Ustedes *Ellos* *Ellas* *(Dos* or *más cosas)*	**están**	You guys **are** They **are** They **are** They **are**
Nosotros(as)	**estamos**	We **are**

Chances are you're already using these action words! If not, here it is in capsule form: ***Estar*** can mean **am, is** or **are** when talking about:
Condition
¿Cómo **está** *usted?*
or
Location
¿Dónde **está** *María?*

See how all forms begin the same?
Est – *oy*
Est – *á*
Est – *án*
Est – *amos*

Knowing these **four** magic words will make the difference!

A closer look at *estar*

• *Estás* is used with *tú*. (It means "You are" among friends or family members.)
• *Esta* without the accent mark (´) means "This." *Esta es una mesa*. This is a table.
• "Think" a bit before you use them. Put your words together just as you do in *inglés!*
  I am happy. → ***Yo estoy*** *contento*. (**condition**)
  The chair **is** over there. → *La silla* **está** *allí*. (**location**)
• Check back on "*Es* versus *Está*"!

Take *un momento* to read the next few pages with care!

Ser

The other "to be" word is **ser** and it's BIG-TIME!

See how weird it is! You'll just have to watch closely. Trust me. It's worth it!

soy   I'm
es   you're, he's, she's, it's
son   they're, you guys are
somos   we're

Instead of location or condition *ser* words relate to:

- *the time*
- *names*
- *origin*
- *occupation*
- *nationality*
- *description*

Check out these examples:

Soy Tony.   Es italiano.   Somos dentistas.

Es de oro.   Son amigos.

Son las dos.   Es grande.   Soy de Los Angeles.

Es de día.   Es una enchilada.

Son para Susana y Roberto.

To Be or Not To Be

Estar

For location and condition (at this moment).

Ser

For everything else!

¡Atención!

Look closely amigos—you've only got **eight words** to remember! and *they don't ever change*.

estoy   soy

está   es

están   son

estamos   somos

HOT TIPS!

- To ask questions, simply add question marks before and after.
  María es bonita.
  Mary is pretty.
  ¿María es bonita?
  Is Mary pretty?
- Or, if you'd like, the subject in question can be moved to the end:
  ¿Es bonita María?
  (Word order in Spanish won't really hurt the message.)
- The informal "you" form of *ser* is *eres*.

Notice the *difference!*

Estar
Yo **estoy aquí**.   I'm here.
Ella **está** *bien*.   She's fine.
Mis amigos **están** *ocupados*.   My friends are busy.
Nosotros **estamos** *trabajando*.   We're working.

Ser
Yo **soy** *Tony*.   I'm Tony.
Ella **es** *cubana*.   She's Cuban.
Mis amigos **son** *altos*.   My friends are tall.
Nosotros **somos** *dentistas*.   We're dentists.

DO IT NOW!

By fooling around with these ASAP, gringos can immediately begin sending complete messages. Back up a few pages and reread. You'll be amazed at how much better your Spanish will be!

TRY SOME!

1. *Tony* **está** *en la casa*.
2. *Ellos* **son** *inteligentes*.
3. *Yo* **estoy** *bien*.
4. **Somos** *cubanos*.
5. **Estamos** *muy contentos*.
6. **Soy** *el presidente*.
7. _____
8. _____
9. _____
10. _____

Just Say No!

What is truly *magnífico* about *español* is that there are so many shortcuts to success! As we've seen, to say *"not"* in Spanish, it's *no* big deal. Do *nothing* more than place a *no* in front of whatever you're trying to say.

*La rata **es** muy grande.*
*La rata **no es** muy grande.*

And *no* matter how complex the action, to say "not" just say, *no!*
*Ella **no** quiere leer libros y escribir ejercicios.*
(She does **not** want to read books and write exercises!)

Take a second to scan these **muy** useful *no-no's*:

No ...   *hay.*   There **isn't** or **aren't** any.
importa.   It's **not** important.
me interesa.   **I'm** not interested.
le haga caso.   **Don't** pay any attention.
me dí cuenta.   I **didn't** realize.
lo aguanto.   I **can't** stand it.
se preocupe.   **Don't** worry.
sabía.   I **didn't** know.
puede ser.   It **can't** be.
me gusta.   I **don't** like it.

Now, what can you learn about action words from these examples? That's right. The "o" ending refers to "I."

No puedo   I can't.
No tengo   I don't have ...
No veo   I can't see.
No necesito   I don't need ...

No quiero   I don't want ...
No recuerdo   I don't remember.
No encuentro   I can't find ...

HOT TIP!

In Spanish, you need a **double no**: *¿Está Juan?—No, no está.* (Is John there? No, he is not.) For words like *nadie* (nobody), put *No* in front of verb: *No está nadie.* (Nobody is here.)

Let's *Tengo!*

Here's another "power play" *en español*—and truly a *must* for the rookie. Whenever you'd like to talk about **who has** what, use the action word *tener* (to have).

Remember: you can delete the *quién* words if you like.

tengo and *tiene* are great for requests and chit-chat.
    *¿**Tiene** cambio?*   Do you have change?
    ***Tengo** dos hermanos.*   I have two brothers.

Tenemos (**We** have) and *tienen* (**you guys** or **they** have) are also nice to know.

TENER   to have

---

*Yo **tengo***	I **have**	*Ustedes*		
		Ellos	*tienen*	You, They **have**
Usted		*Ellas*		
Ella	*tiene* You, He, She **has**			
Él		*Nosotros*	*tenemos* We **have**	
		Nosotras		

TENER can also mean *to be* in the following situations:
    Tengo la culpa.   I'm at fault.   *Tengo razón.*   I'm right.
    Tengo hambre.   I'm hungry.   *Tengo frío.*   I'm cold.
    Tengo sed.   I'm thirsty.   *Tengo calor.*   I'm hot.
    Tengo miedo.   I'm scared.   *Tengo sueño.*   I'm sleepy.
    Tengo suerte.   I'm in luck.   *Tengo 18 años.*   I'm 18 years old.

See how these make great one-liners. And they all work with the other forms of **TENER** just as well:
    Tenemos miedo.   We're scared.
    ¿Tiene frío?   Are you cold?
    Tienen hambre.   They're hungry.

… Here you go! Make some of your own:

_____

_____

_____

"What Are You Doing?" (¿*Qué está haciendo?*)

Acción words in Spanish are usually learned in a predictable order. First, the commands are picked up along with the "to be" words, **ser** and **estar**. Second come the action words referring to "now!" (I call this the **"-ing"** or **-ndo** form.) It's the easiest form to remember and to use. All that's needed is an *acción* word. To say "talking" for example, simply change *hablar* (talk) to *hablando:*

habla**r** → habla**ndo**
(talk)   (talk**ing**)

The **-ndo** replaces the **-r**. All Spanish action words end in *-r*, so the *-ndo* or *-ing* form is *muy simple!*

- *trabajar*   *trabaj**ando***
  work   work**ing**

- *comprar*   *compr**ando***
  buy   buy**ing**

- *manejar*   *manej**ando***
  drive   driv**ing**

> **NOTE**
> Some *acción* words end in *-er* or *-ir* so you have to change the ending to **-iendo** instead of **-ando**:
> - *comer*   *comi**endo***
>   eat   eating
>
> - *escribir*   *escribi**endo***
>   write   writing

And here's how they work:

> **Estamos trabajando** *en el garaje.*
> **We're working** in the garage.
>
> **Estoy comiendo** *con mis amigos.*
> **I'm eating** with my friends.

HOT TIPS!

- Relax! All you need to remember is either **ando** or **iendo**.
- And to "complete" your message, just put the *estar* words in front: "Maria **is** working." becomes *María* **está** *trabajando.*

Onward with ...*ndo*

The key to *real* fluency is to acquire as many *acción words as* possible. Try "fooling around" with these words. First, "-ing" 'em with *-ando* or *-iendo!* Then use them to make statements.

correr (run)	*Ellos están corriendo.*	They're running.
caminar (walk)	*Estoy caminando.*	I'm walking.
salir (leave)	*El tren está saliendo.*	The train is leaving.

abrir open	*jugar* play	*pagar* pay
aprender learn	*limpiar* clean	*parar* stop
beber drink	*lavar* wash	*poner* put
besar kiss	*llegar* arrive	*tirar* throw
cerrar close	*llevar* carry	*vender* sell
empujar push	*llorar* cry	*viajar* travel
jalar pull	*mostrar* show	*volver* return

Ready, Set ...

At this stage of the guidebook, most of you have already started to race forward, constantly in search of *más palabras de acción.*
You have found that knowing how to use the *-ndo* form changes everything. After jabbering a couple of *acciones*, along with some *vocabulario básico*, you have begun to feel like a native speaker. However, before you volunteer as a tour guide, let's first take a look at a few more secrets to understanding those action words!

Beyond ...*ndo*

There's no way that beginning "Spanish-speakers" can pick up all the different action word forms right away. However, after the "*-ndo*'s," it is possible to "shortcut" your way through some of the other grammar junk.

Here is a *grupo* of goodies that will help! You can put these phrases **in front of** action words.

Hay que (One must) …   *traba**jar.*** (work.)
Me gusta (I like) …   *com**er.*** (eat.)
Favor de (Please) …   *escri**bir.*** (write.)
Tengo que (I have to) …
Debo (I should) …
Prefiero (I prefer to) …
Necesito (I need to) …
Puedo (I can) …
Deseo (I wish to) …
Quiero (I want to) …
Quisiera (I'd like to) …

HOT TIP!

You'll be hearing folks add *-ado* or *-ido* to action words instead of *-ndo*. Don't worry about it. It usually means that the action has been completed. *¿Entend**ido**? (Understood?) Remember:* Action words have only three basic endings, (**-ar, -er,** and **-ir**).

Se

A small number of *palabras de acción* have **se** attached. Don't get excited! It simply means that the action is one that *we do to ourselves*. Here's how they work.

lavar is "to wash."

lavarse means "to wash oneself." To *"-ndo,"* say—*lavándose* (washing oneself).

Add *estar* and it's, *Él está lavándose.* (He's washing himself.)

Check out some *más!*

- *acostarse*　lie down
  Nosotros estamos acostándonos.　We're ly**ing** down.
- *bañarse*　bathe oneself
  Ella está bañándose.　She's tak**ing a bath**.
- *cepillarse*　brush one's hair
  Yo estoy cepillándome.　I'm brush**ing** my hair.
- *levantarse*　raise oneself up
  Yo estoy levantándome.　I'm gett**ing** up.
- *peinarse*　comb one's hair
  Juan está peinándose.　John's comb**ing** his hair.
- *sentarse*　sit down
  Ellos están sentándose.　They're sitt**ing** down.

Here's what all these words look like together!
lavarse　wash oneself

Estoy lavándome　　　　　　　*Está lavándose*
Están lavándose　　　　　　　*Estamos lavándonos*

NOTE
• To say "I'm doing it to myself," use *me*.
• To say "We're doing it to ourselves," use *nos*.

CHOOSE 'N USE!

- *¿Quién está …?*　Who is … (bathing, standing up, etc.)?
- *Estoy … ahora mismo.*　I am (lying down, etc.) right now.
- *Estamos … y …*　We are … (combing) and … (brushing our hair).

lo, la le, les, me, nos

Understanding these little pieces of Spanish is easier than using them correctly. So for now, here's what they mean *when used with* action words!

lo; la   it
le   you, him, her
les   you guys, them
me   me
nos   us

Here's what they look like in normal conversation:
Me lo dijo.   He told it to me.
Lo tengo.   I have it.
Nos escribe.   He writes to us.
Pregúntele.   Ask him.

And notice how they usually require the "Reversal Rule"!

La	*La estoy limpiando.* I am cleaning it.
Lo	*Juan lo está haciendo.* Juan is doing it.
Le	*Le están escribiendo.* They are writing you (or him, her).
Les	*Les estamos diciendo.* We are telling them.
Me	*María me está besando.* Maria is kissing me.
Nos	*Ella nos está enseñando.* She is teaching us.

This is not easy. Even native Spanish speakers sometimes have problems with these little devils! But don't let them bother you—for now, just be aware of their general meaning and importance.

HOT TIPS!

- Some action words in the *se* category also change when you *"-ndo"!*
- Let's face it, *se* is strange and needs a little explanation. But *don't let it slow you down!* There are too few *se actions* to worry about.
- You'll also hear *te*, which is informal for "you."
¡Te amo!
I love you!

Here are more of those practical, everyday *palabras de acción* you **really can use** all the time!

Don't forget!
-er, -ir = **iendo**;
-ar = **ando**!

adivinar	guess	*jugar*	play
ahorrar	save	*juntar*	join
amar	love	*montar*	ride
apostar	bet	*nadar*	swim
aprovechar	take advantage	*odiar*	hate
arreglar	arrange	*olvidar*	forget
asistir	attend	*perder*	lose
bailar	dance	*pesar*	weigh
buscar	look for	*pescar*	fish
cantar	sing	*platicar*	chat
celebrar	celebrate	*prestar*	lend
cocinar	cook	*probar*	try
contestar	answer	*quebrar*	break
cortar	cut	*quitar*	take away
dar	give	*recibir*	receive
desarollar	develop	*renunciar*	quit
descansar	rest	*reparar*	fix
desear	wish	*sobrevivir*	survive
disfrutar	enjoy	*soñar*	dream
empezar	begin	*subir*	climb
encontrar	find	*terminar*	finish
escuchar	listen	*tocar*	touch
evitar	avoid	*traducir*	translate
gastar	spend	*usar*	use
gritar	yell	*viajar*	travel
		volar	fly

HOT TIPS!

- It's very likely that you're going to hear many action words that *mean the same* as those listed here! Learn those, too—in case you're "in a bind."
- Some action words have two or more useful meanings: *ganar* (win, earn); *tomar* (take, drink); *hacer* (do, make); *pegar* (hit, stick); *dejar* (leave behind, allow); *pasar* (pass, happen).
- Most commonly used action words end in -*ar*, so use the "-*ando*'s" first!
- Don't worry about spellings now. Speak first!

CHOOSE 'N USE!

- *Mi amigo está …*   My friend is … (yelling, fishing, etc.).
- *Los niños están …*   The children are … (guessing, etc.).
- *Yo estoy … mucho.*   I am … (chatting, etc.) a lot.
- *Nosotros no estamos …*   We are not … (flying, riding, etc.).
- *¿Ustedes están …?*   Are you guys … (listening)?
- *El Sr. Gómez está … y …*   Mr. Gomez is … (swimming) and … (climbing).

Las Acciones Locas

No doubt you have some questions about a few action words that don't seem to perform like the others. I call them *"las locas"* (the "crazies"). Let's take a look at a few of my favorites:

ir (to go)

What's *fantástico* about *ir* is that it tells:
• where you're **"going to"** and
• what you're **"going to"** do later

Learn these words:
Voy a (I'm "going to") … *México.*
Va a (You're, He's, She's "going to") … *mi casa.*
Van a (You guys, They are "going to") … *trabajar.*
Vamos a (We're "going to") … *comer.*

Saber and conocer (To know)

Saber and *conocer* both mean to know, but here's how they differ:
saber *(sé, sabe, saben, sabemos)* means "to know something."
conocer *(conozco, conoce, conocen, conocemos)* means "to know someone."

*Yo **sé** mucho español.*   I know a lot of Spanish.
*Yo **conozco** a muchas personas.*   I know a lot of people.

> Each action word has four basic forms:
> *sé; conozco* (I know)
> *sabe; conoce* (you, he, she knows)
> *saben; conocen* (they, you guys know)
> *sabemos; conocemos* (we know)

"What happened?" (¿Qué pasó?)

There are tons more. Buy a Spanish textbook if you want to learn *más!*

Unfortunately, in Spanish, telling someone about previous events can be done several ways, depending upon your meaning. These are learned gradually when exposed consistently to lots of *español*. So, for the *momento,* let's view a few common "past" words that can help you ASAP!

Dijo   said (you, he, she)
Fue   went (you, he, she)
Comí   ate (I)
Tenía   used to have (I, you, he, she)
Iba   was going (I, he, she); were going (you)

Estaba is the *"was"* word! It is used to talk about past action.
*¿Qué es**taba** haciendo?*   What *were* you doing?
Try these words:

Yo	*estaba*	I was
Usted	*estaba*	You were
Ella	*estaba*	She was
Él	*estaba*	He was
Ellos	*estaban*	They were
Ustedes	*estaban*	You guys were
Nosotros	*estábamos*	We were

CHOOSE 'N USE!
- *¿Conoce usted a …?*   Do you know … (Mary, Tom, etc.)?
- *Trabajo en …*   I work at the … (store, bank, etc.).
- *No estaban …*   They weren't … (working, eating, etc.).
- *Él no sabe …*   He doesn't know the … (name, number, etc.).
- *Fue a …*   He, She went to … (Japan, Europe, etc.).

Bueno, before we *"stop* the action," here's some helpful "inside info" on Spanish *acciones* y *actividades.*

- The worlds of Spanglish and slang have produced countless action words that can be heard daily, particularly in those areas of this country where lots of both Spanish and English are spoken. Try some! (Many sound the same in English.) And of course, *make sure you understand what you're saying.* Use your *best* judgment!

NOTE
- They go great with the *-ndo's.* Also there are only three words to recall; not four!
- **Beware!** There are other **"was"** words.
- Believe me, this **"was" word** will get you going. You can finally start talking about the past!
Ella estaba aquí ayer. She **was** here yesterday.
Estábamos trabajando anoche. We **were** working last night.
Yo no estaba en casa. I **wasn't** home.
¿Estaban jugando ellos? **Were** they playing?

- Read *español.* This is perhaps one of the best ways to learn the various action word forms (tenses). You'll soon be picking up and using stuff that used to take GRINGOS years to learn!

- Notice that action words in *español* have the same form for **we**! No matter what you're trying to say, the (*we*) ending is **-mos**.

	*so**mos.***	**We** are.
Nosotros …	*baila**mos.***	**We** dance.
	*comi**mos.***	**We** ate.

The "you guys" or "they" ending is also easy to remember. Listen for the **n**.

Ellos …	*so**n.***	**They** are.
	*baila**n.***	**They** dance.
Ustedes …	*comiero**n.***	**You guys** ate.

These are only a couple of *muchos* patterns that remain consistent among Spanish action words. So pay attention! You are bound to discover many more.

- There's a unique set of words in Spanish that really go *bien* with the *palabras de acción.* They tell "**how** we do things." What's nice is they all end in **-mente**. (I call 'em the "-ly words." Notice how much they look like *inglés!*)

*breve**mente***	brief**ly**	*perfecta**mente***	perfect**ly**
*correcta**mente***	correct**ly**	*rápida**mente***	rapid**ly**
*efectiva**mente***	effective**ly**	*sincera**mente***	sincere**ly**
*inmediata**mente***	immediate**ly**	*usual**mente***	usual**ly**

And here's how they work:
*Juan está trabajando **rápidamente.***   Juan's working rapidly.
*Estoy hablando **sinceramente.***   I'm talking sincerely.
*Estamos jugando **perfectamente.***   We're playing perfectly.
***Usualmente** no hay problemas.*   Usually, there aren't any problems.

¿Puede recordarlo?
(Can You Remember It?)

- Give a few commands in Spanish.
- Make three different statements using the word *estoy*.
- Make three different statements using the word *soy*.
- Ask a question using the word *tiene*.
- Make a statement using the word *hablando*.
- Name five basic verbs in Spanish.
- Make a statement using the word *estaba*.
- What does *perfectamente* mean?

8

CHAPTER *OCHO*
Los detalles
(Details)

Tell Me When!

We've become familiar with some of these "when" words already. But now—with our knowledge of *¿Cuándo?* (and some *palabras básicas*)—it's *time* to present the most popular words and phrases referring to **el tiempo**. (Recognize any of these one-liners?)

ahora　now; nowadays
ahorita　right now
a la madrugada　at dawn
a la puesta del sol　at sunset
anoche　last night
anteayer　the day before
　yesterday
antes　before
apenas　just
a veces　sometimes
ayer　yesterday
cada día　each day
casi nunca　seldom
después　afterward
entonces　then
esta noche　tonight
hace dos años　two years ago
hasta　until
hoy　today
luego　later

mañana　tomorrow
mañana por la mañana
　tomorrow morning
el mes pasado　last month
muchas veces　lots of times
nunca　never
pasado mañana　the day after
　tomorrow
pronto　soon
la próxima semana　next week
el próximo mes　next month
la semana pasada　last week
siempre　always
tarde　late
temprano　early
todavía　yet
todos los días　every day
una vez　once
un momento　a moment
un rato　awhile
ya　already

CHOOSE 'N USE!
• *Trabajo …*　I work … (today, always, etc.).
• *Estoy trabajando …*　I'm working … (right now, late, etc.).
• *Estaba trabajando …*　I was working … (yesterday, then, etc.).
• *He trabajado …*　I've worked … (before, every day, etc.).
• *Voy a trabajar …*　I'm going to work … (tomorrow, next month, etc.).

Tell Me Where!

Many "location" words were introduced earlier. The subsequent phrases and words allow us to express *exactly* where something (or someone) is located.

With these little beauties, you can answer almost any *¿Dónde?* question. They're OK alone, but they're better in sentences. (You'd be *lost* without them.)

abajo de	down	*debajo de*	under
adentro; dentro de	inside	*desde*	from
afuera; fuera de	outside	*detrás de*	behind
al fondo de	at the bottom	*en*	in, on, at
al lado de	next to	*encima de*	above
a lo largo de	along	*enfrente de*	in front of
alrededor de	around	*entre*	between
arriba de	up	*hacia*	towards
cerca de	near	*lejos de*	far from
contra	against	*sobre*	over

HOT TIPS!

- Create ways to practice these words with commands.
- *Acerca de* means "about" and shouldn't be confused with *cerca de* (near).
- *Reminder:* **estar** tells "where"

CHOOSE 'N USE!
- *Voy a ponerlo ... las cajas.*   I'm going to put it ... (inside, above, etc.) the boxes.
- *La oficina está ... las tiendas.*   The office is ... (near, next to, etc.) the stores.
- *El ratón está corriendo ... ellos.*   The mouse is running ... (toward, under, etc.) them.

Super "where" words!
cualquier parte	anywhere
por algún lugar	somewhere
por ningún lado	nowhere
por todas partes	everywhere

Here's how to "put together" these new words with others you've learned. (The word-joining process is a lot like that of *inglés*).
*El sofá está **enfrente de** la mesa.*   The sofa is in front of the table.

The Wimpy Wonder Words

Cosas grandes often come in small packages. In Spanish, there are a handful of tiny words which can be heard often because of their extreme importance. (You have to listen closely!)

	mí	(me)
	usted	(you)
en (in, on, at) …	*él*	(him)
de (from, of) …	*ella*	(her)
a (to) …	*ellos*	(them)
para (for) …	*ustedes*	(you guys)
por (by, through) …	*nosotros*	(us)

_____(name of person, place, or thing)

And watch for these "Wee wonders!"

sin   without
con   with; check the changes:
  • *con*migo   with me
  • *con*sigo   with you, him, her, them
  • *con*tigo   with you (between friends, family)

See how the *¿quién?* words change slightly when followed by "where" words!

HOT TIP!

Blend 'em together! *a* and *de* always mesh with *el*:
del Soy **del** pueblo.   I'm **from** town.
al Voy **al** parque.   I'm going **to** the park.

Get It Together —Part II

No more fooling around. It's time for the amateurs to step aside. This stuff is for the "pros" only!

Now that action words have been introduced, let's see what they look like when we combine them with all the other stuff. The key is to continue building strings of words—much like we do in English—but without fear of making mistakes!

Here's a simple formula:

La persona + *La acción* + *Lugar* + *Tiempo* = *¡Mucho español!*
  person   action   place   time

Roberto está trabajando en la tienda ahorita.
 Robert   is   working in the store right now.

To elaborate, add **descripción** and *detail!*

Mi amigo Roberto está trabajando en la tienda nueva hoy con María.
My friend Robert is working at the new store today with Maria.

Mis amigos americanos, Bob y Ed, no están trabajando mucho en la tienda nueva, porque ellos tienen clases todos los días.
My American friends, Bob and Ed, aren't working a lot at the new store, because they have classes every day.

Try mixing the order of your phrases.

Tengo el brazo quebrado y el sábado no puedo jugar en el parque con las otras muchachas.
I have a broken arm, and I can't play at the park with the other girls on Saturday.

Or, how about forming a *pregunta?*

¿Su hermana va a la tienda y va a comprar la comida para la cena y los dulces para los niños?
Is your sister going to the store and is she going to buy food for dinner and candy for the kids?

HOT TIPS!

- A "change" in the word order does not usually affect the meaning of the message!
- When you need to stop and "collect your thoughts," why not mutter a word, such as *¡Momento!* (one moment).

There isn't a thing you can't talk about!

Un elefante gordo estaba bañándose en el río ayer y estaba comiendo las plantas debajo del agua.
A fat elephant was bathing in the river yesterday and was eating the plants under the water.

When you get *bueno* at combining your Spanish words, the *el* and *la* Business, the Reversal Rule and the Once-and-for-all Rule will be applied without effort—automatically! Just remember, the more you "babble," the better you'll be!

Also, lengthen those commands! Check back on the *mandatos* and "add on" a few *palabras:*

¡Hable!   Speak!
¡Hable con María!   Speak with Mary!
… add some more:
¡Hable con María en la oficina!   Speak with Mary in the office!

And don't forget to combine two or more commands with the little linkers—*de, a, para, sin,* and *con:*
¡Vaya a la escuela y ***hable*** con María en la oficina!*
Go to the school and **speak** with Mary in the office.

NOTE
Please say *Por favor.*

RSVP

As your strings of *palabras* get longer you'll need techniques to help you over any minor hurdles that may impede communication. Instead of walking away from a good conversation, try the RSVP (*R*epeat, *S*lur, *V*isualize, *P*ause) method of keeping things going. RSVP works, so master it *lo más pronto posible* (as soon as possible).

Repeat it!
- Repeating what you hear is still one of the best ways to acquire language while conversing. Hearing and saying (instead of doing nothing at all) new words more than once, make comprehension and speech that much easier. *¿Comprende?* ***¡Comprende!***

Slur it!
- As ridiculous as it may seem, while you're learning Spanish, one very safe way to stay in a conversation is to slur and mumble those words, or parts of words, that you're not sure of. Using English, Spanglish, and even "creating" your own Spanish words are also very effective ways to reduce your "drop-out" rate.

HOT TIP!

- Spanish mutterings are like those in English, so put two or three *in a row!* Well ... let's see ... OK!

Visualize it!
- When listening or speaking, just *picture* the unfamiliar words in their written form! Since Spanish is always pronounced exactly like it is spelled, comprehension is easy. Try it and you'll SEE!

And are you still using the other "visualization" technique? Keep playing those *word-picture* association games. Here are two of my favorites:

libro (book)   looks like *library*
cuartos (rooms)   looks like *quarters*

P-a-u-s-e it!
- For those moments of silence when you're desperately trying to recall words and form a response, try muttering these life savers!

... *a ver* ...	Let's see ...	... *este* ...	Uh ...
... *o sea* ...	What I mean is ...	... *bueno* ...	OK ...
... *es decir* ...	That is to say ...	... *pues* ...	Well ...

Not Much More to Fluency!

9

CHAPTER *NUEVE*

¡Bienvenidos!

(Welcome ... to the Majors!)

¿Quiere jugar?
("Wanna Play?")

Americans love sports and recreation. And so do many Spanish speakers worldwide. For the Latin American, soccer is the king of sports. (They call it *fútbol.*) *El béisbol* is popular as well; in fact, if you need "listening practice," many ball games are broadcasted on the internet, TV, and radio in both English and Spanish. As for individual hobbies (*pasatiempos*) in Latin America, they vary from person to person, just as they do in the United States. So, which of the following Spanish words might be helpful to you in *your* spare time?

Keep in mind, many sound like *inglés!*

el básquetbol	basketball
el béisbol	baseball
el boliche	bowling
el boxeo	boxing
el fútbol	soccer
el fútbol americano	football
el tenis	tennis
el vólibol	volleyball

el hockey; el surf; el golf
Guess their meaning!

And here are some action words in the games category:

correr	to run
esquiar	to ski
montar a caballo	to ride on horseback
navegar	to sail
patinar	to skate
pescar	to fish

CHOOSE 'N USE!

- *¿Le gusta … o …?*   Do you like … (baseball, etc.) or … (football, etc.)?
- *No sé mucho de …*   I don't know much about … (fishing, checkers, etc.).
- *… es excelente para su salud.*   … (Tennis, running, etc.) is great for your health.
- *Necesitamos …*   We need the … (net, ball, etc.).

HOT TIPS!

- Learn *más* from folks you play with!
- Find out what hobbies are common to folks in Spanish-speaking countries.

How about these "winners"!

¿Juega Ud. tenis?   Do you play tennis?   *¿Cuántos tantos?*   What's the score?

¿Quién ganó?   Who won?   *¿Quién perdió?*   Who lost?

el atleta athlete	*el juego* game	*las pesas* weights
el campo field	*el partido* match	*el ejercicio* exercise
la cancha court	*la pelota* or *la bola* ball	*la canasta* basket
el entrenador coach	*la práctica* practice	*el guante* mitt
el equipo team	*la raqueta* racket	*el bate* bat
el estadio stadium	*la red* net	*el anfiteatro* arena
el gimnasio gymnasium	*el uniforme* uniform	

Mi **pasatiempo** *favorito*   (My favorite **hobby**)

el ajedrez   chess
el dibujo   drawing
la fotografía   photography
el juego de damas   checkers
la lectura   reading
las monedas   coins
los naipes or *las cartas*   cards
el póker   poker
el rompecabezas   puzzle
los sellos   stamps
escuchar música   to listen to music
mirar vídeos   to watch videos
usar la computadora   to use the computer

Jugar con los juguetes (Play with Toys)

Besides *los juegos* (games), we all grow up *jugando con* (playing with) toys. Kids of all ages will want to know the Spanish words for some of the common play *cosas!*

el animal de peluche
  stuffed animal
las caricaturas   cartoons
los chistes   jokes
los colores   crayons
la cometa   kite
los cubos   blocks
el disfraz   costume
la figura de acción   action toy
los fuegos   fireworks
el globo   balloon
la magia   magic
la muñeca   doll
los patines   skates
la patineta   skateboard
la pelota   ball
el rompecabezas   puzzle
los trucos   tricks

HOT TIP!

For a "toy" *object*, it's *tren de juguete* Toy train.

A theatrical play in Spanish has nothing to do with the word "play." It is an *obra de teatro* (a theater work). Yet, if *el drama* is your thing, maybe you can use these words below:

el ceño   frown
chistoso   funny
la comedia   comedy
la diversión   fun
las lágrimas   tears
la risa   laughter
la sonrisa   smile
la tragedia   tragedy

To play a musical instrument requires **tocar** (to touch) instead of *jugar*. Check out how *tocar* sounds when combined with these popular *instrumentos musicales* (musical instruments):

Toca …
You play, He or She plays …

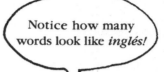

Notice how many words look like *inglés!*

el piano	piano	
el violín	violin	
la guitarra	guitar	
el saxofón or *el saxófono*	saxophone	
la trompeta	trumpet	
el tambor	drum	
el clarinete	clarinet	
el trombón	trombone	
el órgano	organ	

CHOOSE 'N USE!
- *Mi hijo quiere …*   My kid wants … (a guitar, etc.).
- *Tengo … y …*   I have … (a piano, etc.) and … (a violin, etc.).
- *¿Dónde puedo comprar …?*   Where can I buy … (a clarinet, etc.)?

Travel Treats!

We've already covered a few helpful areas for the traveler; such as transportation, shopping, and restaurant talk. The following collection of words, however, includes "the sweetest" of Spanish *palabras* and *frases*, which will assist not only the experienced *turista*, but the occasional vacationer as well. Let's begin with the "life-savers":

¿A qué distancia?   How far?
¿Cuál autobús?   Which bus?
¿Cuál calle?   Which street?
¿Cuánto tiempo?   How much time?
¿Está incluída(o)?   Is it included?
¿Está listo(a)?   Is it ready?
¿Está ocupada(o)?   Is it taken?
¿Hay agua potable?   Is there drinking water?
¿Puede ayudarme?   Can you help me?
¿Puede recomendar uno?   Can you recommend one?
¿Puedo pagar con esto?   Can I pay with this?
¿Puede repararlo?   Can you fix it?
¿Puedo tener cambio?   Can I have change?

And don't leave home, without …

Dónde está …?
Where's …?

> **NOTE**
> **Use your time-telling skills!**
> • *¿Qué día es hoy?* What day is today?
> • *¿A qué hora?* At what time?

la aduana   customs
el aeropuerto   the airport
el banco   the bank
el camino a …   the road to …
el centro   downtown
el correo   the post office
la estación   the station
el hospital   the hospital
el hotel   the hotel
el mapa   the map
la parada del autobús   the bus stop
el restaurante   the restaurant
el semáforo   signal light
la señal   road sign
el teléfono   the phone
la tienda   the store

Unas personas necesarias
la criada   maid
el dueño   owner
el botones   bellboy
el conserje   concierge
el gerente   manager
el chofer   driver
el guía   guide

NOTE
Pack these words away!
- *las maletas*   suitcases
- *la cámara*   camera
- *la visa*   visa
- *el pasaporte* passport
- *el seguro*   insurance
- *la agencia de viajes* travel agency
- *los puntos de interés* points of interest
- *boleto de ida y vuelta* round-trip ticket

Here's a mixed bag of "Good 'n Plenty":

Quiero (I want) …
Necesito (I need) …
Quisiera (I'd like) …

hacer reservaciones (to make reservations)
cargarlo (to charge it)
pagarlo (to pay it)
cambiarlo (to exchange it)
hacer una llamada (to make a call)
ordenar (to order)
un boleto (a ticket)
la llave (the key)
un taxi (a taxi)
más toallas (more towels)
una habitación (a room)
más hielo (more ice)
una bebida (a drink)
la cuenta (the bill)
un corte de pelo (a haircut)
cancelarlo (cancel it)

… por favor!

El carro   (The car)

el aceite oil
el agua water
la batería battery
la gasolina gas
el motor engine
la llanta desinflada flat tire
¡Llénelo! Fill it up!
la maletera trunk

¡La pesca!   (Fishing)

el anzuelo hook
la bahía bay
el bote boat
la caña rod
el carrete reel
el cordel line

la salvavidas lifesaver
la isla island
lanzar to cast
la marea tide
el nudo knot
las olas waves

el pescado fish
el pescador fisherman
pescar to fish
la punta point
la red net
las rocas rocks

¡Márquelo y Suéltelo! **Tag** it and **release** it!

Now, sample these "suckers"!

el alfiler pin
la bolsa bag
la botella bottle
la caja box
la carta letter
la cerradura lock
el champú shampoo
los cigarillos cigarettes
el desodorante deodorant
el enjuague conditioner
los fósforos matches
el hilo thread
el jabón soap

la lata can
la medicina medicine
las navajas razors
el papel higiénico toilet paper
el periódico newspaper
la propina tip
el racado message
la revista magazine
el rollo de película roll of film
el sello stamp
el sobre envelope
la tarjeta postal postcard
la canasta basket

El dinero

Find out the names for the currency and its rate of exchange before you travel anywhere.
Practice pronouncing the words and phrases you'll need for a few days before you leave!

Survival Signs

In traveling, the key to success is *awareness*. So keep your *ojos* open for these common *letreros* (signs) and you won't be "lost."

ABIERTO	Open	*EMPUJE*	Push
ADUANA	Customs	*ENTRADA*	Entrance
ALTO	Stop	*ESTACIONAMIENTO*	Parking
CEDA EL PASO	Yield	*GLORIETA*	Traffic Circle
CERRADO	Closed	*JALE*	Pull
CRUZ ROJA	Red Cross	*NO FUMAR*	No Smoking
DESCOMPUESTO	Out of Order	*SALIDA*	Exit
DESPACIO	Slow	*SANITARIOS*	Restrooms
DESVIACIÓN	Detour	*SE ALQUILA*	For Rent
DIRECCIÓN ÚNICA	One Way	*SE VENDE*	For Sale
EMERGENCIA	Emergency	*VÍA EQUIVOCADA*	Wrong Way

Las medidas (Measurements)
(Study your metrics!)
el litro   liter
el metro   meter
el kilómetro = 5/8 mile
el kilógramo = 2.2 lbs.
$0°C = 32°F$
And ask folks about any abbreviations you see!

CHOOSE 'N USE!

- *Primero vamos a buscar …*   First let's look for the … (passport, bellhop, etc.).
- *¿Qué significa …?*   What does … (customs, for rent, etc.) mean?
- *Présteme …*   Lend me the … (camera, key, etc.).

What's in a *nombre*?

It's amazing how much influence Spanish has had over the years in many parts of the United States. Yet, we seldom stop to ponder the meaning of names of many of our cities, states, and landmarks. Some of them may surprise you.

Alamo   (Poplar tree)   *Nevada*   (Snowfall)
Amarillo   (Yellow)   *Rio Grande*   (Large river)
Colorado   (Red)   *Sacramento*   (Sacrament)
El Paso   (The pass)   *San Antonio*   (Saint Anthony)
Florida   (Flowery)   *San Diego*   (Saint James)
Las Vegas   (The plains)   *San Francisco*   (Saint Francis)
Los Angeles   (The angels)   *Santa Fe*   (Holy Faith)
Montana   (Mountain)   *Sierra*   (Mountain range)

Southwestern Specials

There's one part of the United States that's got *español* literally *everywhere!* Here are words that can be *seen* or *heard* throughout the Southwest:

agua   (water)   *palo*   (stick, stump)
arroyo   (creek)   *playa*   (beach)
costa   (coast)   *puerto*   (port)
loma   (hill)   *real*   (royal)
mar   (sea)   *río*   (river)
mira   (look)   *santa* or *san*   (saint)
misión   (mission)   *valle*   (valley)
monte   (mountain)   *vista*   (view)

• *avenida*   (Avenue)   • *camino*   (Road)
• *calle*   (Street)   • *del*   (of the)

And how about *los nombres de personas!* Obviously, those listed here are only the most prevalent. Yours may or may not have an equivalent. (*Ask around!*)

Male Names

Al   *(Alfredo)*
Bob   *(Roberto)*
Charlie   *(Carlos)*
Ed   *(Eduardo)*
Frank   *(Francisco)*
George   *(Jorge)*
Jim   *(Jaime)*
Joe   *(José)*
John   *(Juan)*
Mark   *(Marcos)*
Mike   *(Miguel)*
Peter   *(Pedro)*
Rick   *(Ricardo)*
Steve   *(Esteban)*
Tom   *(Tomás)*
William   *(Guillermo)*

Female Names

Alice   *(Alicia)*
Ann   *(Ana)*
Barb   *(Bárbara)*
Carol   *(Carolina)*
Debbie   *(Débora)*
Helen   *(Elena)*
Jane   *(Juanita)*
Kathy   *(Catalina)*
Liz   *(Isabel)*
Lynn   *(Lina)*
Marge   *(Margarita)*
Martha   *(Marta)*
Mary   *(María)*
Nancy   *(Anita)*
Sally   *(Sara)*
Susan   *(Susana)*

HOT TIPS!

- Some names are written the same in both languages: David, Samuel, Daniel, Gloria, Linda, Virginia.
- Some have "nicknames":
  Francisco   "Nacho"
  Guillermo   "Memo"
  José   "Pepe"
- And add **-ito** for endearment
  *Juan   "Juan**ito**"*

That's *Amor*

This guidebook would be incomplete without the presentation of the most significant Spanish "love lines." Romance is only a few *palabras* away.

Soy ...   *casado(a)*   married
I'm ...   *soltero(a)*   single
           divorciado(a)   divorced
           viudo(a)   widowed

"Power Lines"

Estoy enamorado(a).   I'm in love.
Es una promesa.   It's a promise.
¿Te gustó?   Did you enjoy it?
Me divertí mucho.   I had a nice time.
¿Puedo verte más tarde?   Can I see you later?
¿Quieres casarte conmigo?   Will you marry me?
¿Quisieras ...   Would you like to ...
   bailar?   dance?
   dar un paseo?   take a walk?
   platicar?   chat?
   salir?   leave?
Te quiero.   I love you.

¿Cómo es?   (What's he, or she, like?)

Es ...
He's or She's ...

agradable pleasant	*honesto(a)* honest
amistoso(a) friendly	*responsable* responsible
apasionado(a) passionate	*romántico(a)* romantic
aplicado(a) studious	*simpático(a)* nice
chistoso(a) funny	*sincero(a)* sincere
celoso(a) jealous	*tímido(a)* shy
cruel mean	
educado(a) well-mannered	• *besos.* kisses XXXX.
fiel faithful	• *abrazos.* hugs OOOO.
guapo(a) handsome	

Nice Things to Say

<u>Girl to boy/Boy to girl:</u>

chulo/a   cute
mi amor   my love
mi corazón   sweetheart
mi dulce   my sweet
mi tesoro   my treasure
mi vida   love of my life
querido/a   darling
precioso/a   precious

<u>Boy to girl only:</u>

bella   beautiful
hermosa   lovely
linda   very pretty
mi reina   my queen
bonita   pretty

• Embrace these words!

los amantes   the lovers
el aniversario   anniversary
la boda   wedding
el cine   movie
el concierto   concert
la fiesta   party
el matrimonio   marriage
los novios   the engaged
la pareja   the couple

• A "date" is *una cita*.

HOT TIP!

Lovers and friends use the word *tú* for "you" instead of *usted*.

CHOOSE 'N USE!
• *¡Él es tan ...!*   He is so ... (cute, romantic, etc.).
• *¡Sí! Pero es muy ... también.*   Yes, but he's very ... (shy, cruel, etc.) also.
• *Mi ..., te quiero tanto.*   My ... (darling, love, etc.), I love you so much.
• *Nos conocimos en ...*   We met at a ... (wedding, concert, etc.).

La religión, la política, y la filosofía

You can guess what *la religión, la política,* and *la filosofía* mean. And although it's better to avoid such controversial topics in any language, there's a chance they may pop up in beginning *conversación.* So if you're interested in the *argumento inevitable,* arm yourself with these fiery fundamental words:

el capitalismo	capitalism	*la justicia*	justice
la cárcel	jail	*la ley*	law
el castigo	punishment	*la libertad*	freedom
el comunismo	communism	*las mentiras*	lies
el crimen	crime	*la minoría*	minority
la cultura	culture	*el partido*	political party
la democracia	democracy	*el pleito*	lawsuit
los derechos	rights	*el público*	public
la economía	economy	*el racismo*	racism
la educación	education	*la salud*	health
la energía	energy	*el tribunal*	courtroom
el gobierno	government	*la verdad*	truth
el juicio	trial	*el voto*	vote

El mundo   (The world)

el aborto	abortion	*la inmigración*	immigration
las armas	weapons	*el medio ambiente*	the environment
el calentamiento global	global warming	*las pandillas*	gangs
el cáncer	cancer	*la paz*	peace
la contaminación	pollution	*la pobreza*	poverty
las drogas	drugs	*el respeto*	respect
la enfermedad	sickness	*el sexo*	sex
el estrés	stress	*el SIDA*	AIDS
el genocidio	genocide	*los terroristas*	terrorists
la guerra	war	*la violencia*	violence
la huelga	strike		

- *amar*   to love
- *odiar*   to hate

Yo creo ...   ("I believe ...")

el ángel angel	*los musulmanes* Moslems
la Biblia Bible	*los santos* saints
los budistas Buddhists	*la Virgen* the Virgin
los católicos Catholics	*el alma* soul
la creación creation	*el cielo* heaven
los cristianos Christians	*la fe* faith
el diablo devil	*el funeral* funeral
Dios God	*el infierno* hell
el Espíritu Santo Holy Spirit	*el milagro* miracle
Jesucristo Jesus Christ	*la muerte* death
los judíos Jews	*la vida* life
los mormones Mormons	

- *¿Qué piensa de ...?*   What do you think of ...?
- *En mi opinión ...*   In my opinion ...
- *Según ...*   According to ...

Whenever heavy topics are discussed, play it safe! Make *comentarios* with those "one-a-day" one-liners!

La cultura hispánica

Language and culture are inseparable. Therefore, it's imperative that we take time to look closely at the people who speak Spanish. Who are they? Where do they come from? What are their values, traditions, and life styles? Only through understanding one's *cultura* can true communication take place. Chatting is fine, but knowing where the speaker is "coming from" makes all the difference. So do a little research. Read up on Puerto Rican customs, Cuban society, or Mexican history. Learn by asking. Find out about family relationships, foods, and traditional holidays. And keep an open mind. Conversations always become more meaningful when there is mutual respect and consideration.

There's no way we can generalize and stereotype Spanish speakers. Folks from Cuba, Puerto Rico, and Mexico are not *all alike*. Sure, they share the same language, but each nation's heritage, diet, and everyday conversations differ in several ways. First, let's check out a few *diferencias*. These are considered popular among folks from Cuba, Puerto Rico, and Mexico:

Cuba

¡No chive!   Don't bother me!
¿Oigo?   Hello? (on phone)
¡Hola mi socio!   Hi, pal!
¡Concho!   Darn!
¡Oye chico, no seas patán!   Hey, don't be a jerk!
Zanjar un asunto.   To solve a problem.
Es un arroz con mango.   It's very complicated.
¡Qué pesado me cae!   I can't stand him!

Puerto Rico

¡Oye, tocayo!   Hey, buddy!
No más.   Nothin' else.
¡Tranca la boca!   Shut up!
Ser la medio guayaba de …   To be …'s wife.
Saltar el charco.   Fly to New York.
¡Ay, bendito!   Dear Lord!
¡Arranca pa'lante!   Let's get going!
¿Me das pon?   Would you give me a ride?
¡Chévere!   Excellent!

Mexico

¿Mande?   How's that?
¡Pásele!   Go ahead!
¿Bueno?   Hello? (on phone)
¡Ay, chihuahua!   Oh, my gosh!
¿Qué traes?   What's new?
¡Vámonos!   Let's go!
¡Dispensa!   Excuse me!
¡Derecho, derecho!   Straight ahead!
¡Qué gacho!   How mean!
¡Ándele!   Hurry up!

Unas palabras básicas …

Cuba

blumers   underwear
espejuelos   glasses
fregar platos   wash dishes
gomas   tires
guagua   bus
haragán   lazy
jimagua   twin
maní   peanuts
mima   mom
mi viejo   my friend
pipo   dad
servicio   toilet
fajarse   to fight
playera   sleeveless T-shirt
pelado   penniless

Mexico

chamaco   kid
charreadas   rodeos
guacamole   avocado sauce
guajolote   turkey
huaraches   sandals
maíz   corn
mariaches   musicians
rancheras   ranch songs
sarape   blanket
tardeadas   afternoon parties
vaqueros   cowboys
chamarra   jacket
llanta ponchada   flat tire
tecolote   owl
gavacho   gringo

Puerto Rico

batey   front yard
bodega   grocery store
chino   orange
caucho   sofa
frisa   blanket
guineo   banana
melón   watermelon
negrito   loved one
papito   daddy
pelea de gallos   cockfight
sombrilla   umbrella
babilla   bravery
chavo   money
compai   pal
temporal   hurricane

Las comidas tradicionales (Traditional Foods)

Here are a few very popular dishes served throughout Mexico, Cuba, and Puerto Rico. *I recommend them all!*

Mexican Food
(Comida mexicana)

barbacoa (BBQ lamb)

birria (shredded goat meat)

bolillos (rolls)

buñuelos (deep fried donuts)

burrito (wrapped and filled flour tortilla)

carne asada (grilled beef strips)

carnitas (roast pork)

chile relleno (stuffed pepper)

enchiladas (usually cheese)

flan (vanilla pudding)

flautas (deep fried taco)

frijoles (beans, of course)

huevos rancheros (eggs with salsa)

lengua (cow's tongue)

menudo (tripe soup)

mole (chicken, turkey, or pork in sauce)

nopales (diced cactus)

pan dulce (Mexican pastry)

pozole (soup with pork)

quesadilla (cheese on tortillas)

sope (small, pizzalike tortilla)

taco (soft, not hard)

tamal (wrapped in corn husk)

tortillas (corn or flour)

tostada (flat and fried)

HOT TIP!

Ask "how" certain foods are eaten, or "how" they are prepared.

Cuban Food *(Comida cubana)*

ajiaco   (vegetable and meat soup)

arroz a la cubana   (white rice and fried egg)

arroz congrí   (rice with black beans)

arroz con leche   (rice, milk, and sugar)

arroz con pollo   (rice with chicken)

boniatos   (sweet potatoes)

chambarete   (lamb shanks)

empanada   (meat pie)

frijoles negros   (black beans)

malanga   (root vegetable)

mojito   (popular drink)

picadillo   (spicy hash)

ropa vieja   (shredded beef)

tostones   (banana chips)

yuca con mojo   (potatolike vegetable)

Puerto Rican Food *(Comida puertorriqueña)*

adobo   (meat marinade)

arañas   (shredded plantains)

arroz con gandules   (exotic rice and bean dish)

arroz guisado   (stew and rice)

arroz y habichuelas rojas   (rice and kidney beans)

bacalao   (pickled codfish)

camarones al ajillo (shrimp in butter sauce)

chayote relleno   (stuffed squash)

gandinga   (pork and kidney stew)

mofongo   (large fried green banana dish)

pasteles   (husk-wrapped dish)

quesito   (cream cheese pastry)

sofrito   (spicy seasoning)

vianda   (starchy vegetables)

¿Puede recordarlo? (Can You Remember It?)

- Name five words that tell "when?"
- Name five words that tell "where?"
- Name five words that relate to sports.
- Name three toys.
- Name five words you may need on a trip.
- Name three words that relate to love.
- Name five words that relate to religion, politics, or philosophy.
- What's you favorite Mexican food?

10

CHAPTER *DIEZ*

Las últimas palabras

(Last Words)

Talk About Language

Eventually, during the Spanish learning experience you will be forced to communicate with the "language" words commonly found in textbooks. (Remember these from English class?)

el adverbio	adverb	*la página*	page
el capítulo	chapter	*las palabras*	words
la conjugación	conjugation	*la práctica*	practice
el diálogo	dialog	*la pregunta*	question
el ejemplo	example	*el pronombre*	pronoun
el ejercicio	exercise	*la pronunciación*	pronunciation
la escritura	the writing	*el repaso*	review
la estructura	structure	*el símbolo*	symbol
el estudio	study	*el significado*	meaning
el examen	test	*el sonido*	sound
la frase	sentence	*el sujeto*	subject
la gramática	grammar	*el sustantivo*	noun
el habla	speech	*la tarea*	homework
el idioma	language	*el tema*	theme
la lección	lesson	*el tiempo*	tense
la lectura	the reading	*el verbo*	verb
la mayúscula	capital letter	*el vocabulario*	vocabulary
el método	the method	*la vocal*	vowel
la minúscula	lower case letter	*la voz*	voice

Things *you* might say:
- *¡El estudio de la gramática no es muy importante!*   The study of grammar is not very important!
- *¡Necesito más práctica y repaso!*   I need more practice and review!
- *¡No me gustan los exámenes y las tareas!*   I don't like tests and homework!
- *¡Comprendo el significado del vocabulario!*   I understand the meaning of the vocabulary!

Práctica, práctica, práctica (Practice!)

Traditionally, foreign language "practice" involved completion of grammar exercises, dialog memorization, and hours of audiolingual drills in a language lab. *Good News!* Practice techniques have changed—and in my opinion, for the better. The following methods are currently being applied worldwide in the most successful programs.

Learning Vocabulario

- Use the **command** words! Combine them with names of things you'd like to know. Use real objects or pictures of items. Have a friend "order you" to touch or move whatever it is you're learning.
- **Interview** Spanish speakers! List items like *sports* or *foods* and ask individuals which ones they like or dislike. Use a question like *¿Le gusta a Ud. …?* (Do you like …?) and check off their responses.
- Collect Spanish children's books, coloring books, or toys. Since you're a "child" in the language, it's important to have lots of **visual exposure** to new words. While reading, point to each picture and "name it" in *español*. (This is really fun to do with the kids!)
- Make an audio **CD.** Ask a native Spanish speaker to read aloud a list of words that you need to know. Record different people, so you can hear all the different sounds. At first, don't bother with vocabulary you're not going to use every day. And offer to make an English CD in return!
- **Draw** pictures of items in special categories, and then **label** them. (The "unartistic," can find pictures on the Internet!)

> **NOTE**
> Although it's not always feasible, these activities work better when learners are assisted by *native* Spanish speakers.

Comidas (Foods)

manzana   *plátano*   *coco*   *melón*

- **Be creative!** For example, practice descriptive words by drawing either a strange-looking monster or your dream date!

muy gordo	mucho dinero
cuatro brazos	muy bonita
tres ojos	muy inteligente
orejas grandes	_____
_____	_____
_____	

La Computadora

Chances are your computer will play a big part in your language learning experience. In Spanish, computer vocabulary is often the same as in English (*el CD-ROM, la DSL, la internet,* etc.). However, these other words might be useful, too:

Voy a ...	I'm going ...
archivar	to file
buscar	to search
conectar	to connect
descargar	to download
eliminar	to delete
encontrar	to find
enviar	to send

escoger	to select
guardar	to save
imprimir	to print
pulsar	to click
recibir	to receive
reenviar	to forward
responder	to reply

¿Dónde está …?	Where's (the) …?
el adjunto	attachment
la basura	trash
el buscador	search engine
el buzón	mailbox
la contraseña	password
el correo electrónico	e-mail address
el mensaje	message
el menú	menu
el navegador	browser
la página inicial	home page
el programa	program
el servidor	server
el sitio web	website

Check out the parts of an e-mail in Spanish!

Tony	**@**	**winner**	**.**	**provider**	**.**	**pe**
nombre del usuario	*arroba*	*nombre de dominio*	*punto*	*el proveedor de acceso a la internet*	*punto*	*el país*
(user name)	(at)	(domain name)	(dot)	(provider)	(dot)	(country)

Notice that *.com, .edu, .org*, etc. are not normal closings to an e-mail in other countries. In many cases, the country such as **.fr** (France), **.es** (Spain), and **.pe** (Peru) each have their own abbreviation.

Learning Basic *Conversaciones*

The best advice I can offer to those wanting experience in basic Spanish chit-chat is: *Just do it!* However, to "practice" conversation on your own, here are two helpful suggestions.

- A fun game one can play with a new language is to "white-out" words from the funnies, and then make up "foreign" responses which relate to the pictures. Use *any* Spanish words you know. (Write it in or just *say it!*)

- On paper, create a dialog of your own—*one that you need* and will use often. With scissors, cut out each one-liner, phrase, and so on; then, mix them up. Practice putting the pieces in order so that it makes sense.

Learning *Acciones*

Unquestionably, the most natural way to acquire action words is by having someone command you "to do something." In acting out the command, you "pick up" on the action word used. On the other hand, with **"visuals,"** you can begin to "talk" about what's going on. And creating your own "visuals" is easy. All you need are some paper, a few old magazines, glue, and a pair of scissors. Use the models given below, or develop your own. Get friends and family involved. Let that imagination run wild! Let's begin with a "visual" that helps teach the *affirmative, negative,* and *question* forms. Try these with *comiendo* (eating).

With a chart, we can expand on the action words!

The visuals can be "read":

a. *Yo **no** estoy comiendo manzanas.*
b. *Sí, ella está comiendo plátanos.*
c. *¿Ellos están comiendo naranjas?*
d. *¡Nosotros _____ _____ _____ _____!*

NOTE: Try creating this visual game on your computer! Find graphics, invent situations, and apply all the vocabulary and verbs you've learned so far.

And this picture-story is for the superstar who already knows a bunch of action words. Go box to box, and tell what's happening in each picture. (When you get really *bueno en español,* you'll be able to answer questions about the story, such as "What happened last night?" or "What happens every day?") You're not that far away.

Learning *"Grammar"*

As in all languages, in Spanish, grammar or "grammatical structure" is acquired "naturally" through trial and error. That's why a child's sentences always sound "so cute." It takes years of mistakes (and hours of classroom instruction) before anyone is able to respond consistently—using "proper grammar." Fortunately, for second-language learners there is a shortcut. Recent studies indicate that reading is one way to "fast and painless" language acquisition. Thus, by reading Spanish, learners can "pick up" basic rules of *la gramática española.* It seems that when GRINGOS read simple, interesting Spanish material regularly, their spoken Spanish improves—and their grammar usage becomes *correcto* most of the time!

The following is a brief story filled with the information introduced in Chapters 3 to 8. Before you read it, go back and skim the chapters. Then, read through the story. Next, check the chapters again to confirm comprehension.

> **NOTE**
> Children's books work very well for this activity. Or, for the more industrious, cut out and paste photos of people in action to light cardboard or construction paper. They make super flash cards!

Una historia **(A Story)**

Yo soy <u>Roberto</u>. Ahora estoy <u>muy bien</u>. Tengo <u>28</u> años y no tengo muchos problemas. Estoy trabajando para una <u>compañía</u> grande en los Estados Unidos con muchos de mis <u>amigos</u>. Me gusta mi trabajo. Me gusta mi familia, también. Todos son de <u>México</u>. En mi casa están mi <u>esposa</u>, mis <u>hijos</u>, mi <u>madre</u> y mi <u>abuelo</u>. La casa es grande. Tiene <u>cuatro</u> dormitorios, <u>tres</u> baños, una cocina <u>grande</u> y la sala. Pero no hay garaje. Es un problema porque tengo un carro <u>nuevo</u>. Es un Toyota <u>blanco</u>.

Mi esposa y mi madre están trabajando ahora en un <u>restaurante</u>. Están muy <u>contentas</u> allí. Mis hijos están estudiando en las escuelas públicas. Son muy inteligentes. Están estudiando el <u>inglés</u>. Mi abuelo no está trabajando porque tiene problemas con su <u>espalda</u>.

El <u>lunes</u> no voy a trabajar. Estoy preparando todo para un viaje a <u>México</u>. Cada <u>diciembre</u> toda la familia tiene una fiesta grande en nuestro pueblo. El pueblo está en <u>las montañas</u>, y es necesario comprar mucha <u>comida</u> y <u>ropa</u> especial. Por ahora estoy trabajando horas extra para pagar por el viaje.

Ahora estoy trabajando "overtime."

The popular close and open-ended techniques are used in stories to teach both grammar and vocabulary. Certain words are deleted, and readers insert any appropriate vocabulary. So "exchange" the underlined words for others! (The same could also be done with the action words!) Personal tales involving daily activities appear to work best.

HOT TIPS!

- Go to the Internet and click "Spanish language" instead of English. You will understand very little at first, but perseverance and imagination will get you far.
- Collect varied Spanish reading materials! In addition to *books, newspapers,* and *magazines*—gather inserts, labels, brochures, flyers, forms, posters, etc. (*Words with pictures* are best.)
- *Librerías* (bookstores), *bibliotecas* (libraries), *papelerías* (stationery stores), and *quioscos* (newsstands) sell or loan out literature for all reading levels. (Browsing in these places is nice—*you don't have to say a word!*)
- Avoid stopping to "study" words and sentences! Calmly skim over what you don't understand and try to focus on the main idea of each paragraph.
- At home, practice reading *aloud.* Tape yourself, play it back, and then note any obvious "soundmaking" problems. (For best results, "read along" with native speakers!)

Unas preguntas para Ud. (Some Questions for You)

Here are 22 common *preguntas* you **should** now be able to answer. (*Por favor*, be brief!)

¿Cómo está usted?
¿Cómo se llama usted?
¿Cuál es su número de teléfono?
¿Quién es su doctor?
¿De quién es este libro?
¿Le gusta a usted la música clásica?
¿Qué hora es?
¿Qué día es hoy?
¿Qué tiempo hace?
¿Cuáles son tres partes del cuerpo?
¿Cuántas hermanas tiene usted?
¿Hay un perro en su casa?
¿Dónde trabaja usted?
¿Es muy bonita la Mona Lisa?
¿Dónde está su cama?
¿Es usted de los Estados Unidos?
¿Tiene usted hambre?
¿Cuántos años tiene usted?
¿Qué está haciendo usted?
¿Qué están haciendo los miembros de su familia?
¿Cuándo habla usted el español?
¿Qué hay detrás de usted?

The Answers?
...Write 'em
or
Just say 'em!
and
sorry, but you'll have to check 'em yourself!

Following are ten preguntas you **might** be able to answer!
¿Sabe usted mucho español?
¿Adónde va usted mañana?
¿Se lava usted las manos todos los días?
¿Quién fue el primer presidente de los Estados Unidos?
¿Dónde estaba usted anoche?
¿Quiere usted ir a Disneylandia?
¿Tiene usted miedo de los gatos negros?
¿Puede usted jugar fútbol?
¿De dónde es usted?
¿Qué hace si ve el letrero "empuje"?

Before I Say *Adiós* ...

Without a doubt, this was the most difficult part of the entire guidebook to write. What more can I say? Everything you really need to get started in Spanish has already been introduced. (I know, because I once was in your *zapatos*.) Nevertheless, to make it all really work, I decided to summarize my thoughts in a series of closing remarks, personal comments and easy-to-follow suggestions which, when considered, lead gringo learners to immediate success in Spanish. *Por favor*, take heed.

Three Big Steps to *Comunicación*

NEXT:

Spanish for Gringos 2 ... and beyond!

(mucho más vocabulario)
Third: You need to use the "*-ndo's*"

(más vocabulario)
Second: You've got to feel good about the verbs *Ser* and *Estar*.

(vocabulario)
First: You've got to know the *"Secrets to Soundmaking"*

Five Things to Always Keep In Mind

1 *Pronunciation* and *grammar* don't matter that much!
2 You don't have to speak until you feel like doing it!
3 Feeling comfortable around non-English speakers makes a difference!
4 You can't make any excuses for not learning!
5 Language learning takes place when you *relax* and have fun!

The Secrets to Success (All of these have already been mentioned. They are all **muy, muy importante**!)

- Try to be sensitive to and aware of cultural differences.
- Get in the habit of using Spanish *regularly*.
- Constantly memorize vocabulary through "word-picture" association.
- Experiment, take chances, and guess when you are unsure!
- Follow the practice tips and activities mentioned throughout *Spanish for Gringos.*
- *Add your own* ideas on how to practice and improve! This guidebook only establishes a base for your entire Spanish learning experience. Ask around, listen, and "build" from here.

Some *más* Advice:

- Try relaxation techniques before you "go for it." Stress-relief literature is available everywhere.
- Don't "stop in the middle" to translate! Whenever you're listening, concentrate on the topic first, so that you have some idea of what's going on.
- Aggressive, outgoing, fun-loving Gringos usually learn Spanish faster than others. A childlike attitude also seems to help!
- When you are in an embarrassing situation, stuck, confused, or at a loss for Spanish words, rely on these for help: *Lo siento.* (I'm sorry.) *No recuerdo la palabra.* (I don't remember the word.) *Estoy estudiando español.* (I'm studying Spanish.)
- Please say *por favor*. In Spanish, you'll go far if you are courteous. The more respectful you are, the more Spanish you'll learn. So practice "polite" things to say. And as always—be sincere.
- Be patient! I know what the word "busy" means—but life's too short to pass up those rare opportunities to practice talking Spanish with someone. Trust me—take the extra moments *now* or later you'll regret not doing so.
- Some words mean *two* or *more* things in Spanish. Find out the appropriate use for each meaning. Dictionaries often help—but be careful! (It's always better to go *straight to the source*.)

NOTE
Do not memorize these rules! Simply be aware of the problems facing the beginner! Remember that "being close" is good enough. Besides, *all* of this stuff is picked up **muy rápido** once you actually get started.

- Memorizing jokes, tongue-twisters, rhymes, and folk songs is a fantastic way to gain confidence while learning language skills.

- Spanish speakers of different countries don't all agree! It's not uncommon for them to "clash" over meanings of words, customs, or historical events. That's why it's important to be aware of the differences between Hispanic dialects. Try to be good at guessing where folks are from!

The Gringo Nightmares (*Problemas* we all seem to have!)

- **The Secrets to Soundmaking**   Even though pronunciation doesn't need to be practiced, becoming familiar with the "*Big Five* and the *Others*" will definitely make understanding and speaking a whole lot easier. (In particular, watch out for the *e, a,* and *i*!) Remember, in Spanish you *always pronounce the letters the same. There are no exceptions!*
- **The *EL* and *LA* Business**   Again, although it won't effect communication much, practice putting **la** in front of objects ending with **a**, and **el** before those ending with **o**. (You'll just have to remember which one goes with words *not* ending in **o** or **a**.)
- **The Reversal Rule**   When describing things, giving the date, or telling "whose," *think backward!* In these instances, the Spanish word order is "reversed."
- **The Once-and-for-All Rule**   Another pattern that should be mentioned is the way in which strings of words have to "agree" in Spanish. "Agreement" is best understood by observing some examples. Notice how the words "agree" with each other:

  Los libros buenos   The good books
  La muchacha bonita   The pretty girl
  Muchas casas negras y blancas   Lots of black and white houses

¡Mini-problemas!

Here are a handful of **palabras** that always seem to bother the GRINGO learner. Pay close attention—they're "sneaky":

poquito a little bit
pequeño small in size

muy very
mucho a lot

número number
nombre name

que that
qué what

dólar dollar
dolor pain

sí yes
si if

esta this one
está is

de nada you're welcome
nada nothing

grande big
largo long

bueno good
bien well

jueves Thursday
huevos eggs

hombre man
hambre hunger

nuevo new
nueve nine

casa house
cosa thing

Add some of your own!

_____   _____

_____   _____

Últimas palabras (Final Words)

It's entirely up to you how much *español* you'll eventually speak and understand. I hope that the easy-to-follow format has made your learning experience enjoyable—free of the stress and frustration of traditional programs. And probably by now you've discovered how the guidebook can be used to get best results. Use *Spanish for Gringos* any way you'd like! Set your own pace, take what you need, and reread only those pages that interest you. Some degree of language acquisition is guaranteed.

But this is really only the beginning. At the moment, you're merely crawling, standing, or staggering in the language. Trust me, fellow gringos, the best is yet to come.

Su amigo,

Bill

GUIDE TO SPANISH SOUNDMAKING

A Quick-check Reference to Basic Pronunciation

- Spanish words are pronounced exactly the way they are written.
- Knowing the BIG 5 (vowels) is the key to speaking and understanding Spanish.
- Poor pronunciation in Spanish does not seriously effect communication, so do the best you can.
- Turn up the volume for the accented (´) parts of words. Spanish words without accents get more volume at the end, *unless* they end in A, E, I, O, U, N, or S. These get more volume on the *next to the last part.*
- Spanish words are "run-together" in short, choppy pieces, usually pronounced in the front part of the mouth, with little or no air being used to make the sounds.

Exercises

Connect each word with its correct translation:

Colors	Los colores	The class	La clase
black	*morado*	book	*pluma*
green	*rojo*	pencil	*papel*
white	*verde*	paper	*libro*
purple	*negro*	table	*lápiz*
red	*blanco*	pen	*mesa*

Expressions	Las expresiones		
Good idea	*Quizás*	It's true	*Yo tampoco*
Me, too	*Creo que sí*	I'm so glad	*Con razón*
Maybe	*Sin duda*	No doubt	*Me alegro*
I think so	*Yo también*	Me, neither	*Es verdad*
No wonder	*Buena idea*	That's OK	*Está bien*

Questions	Las preguntas
What?	*¿Dónde?*
How much?	*¿Quién?*
Where?	*¿Qué?*
Who?	*¿Cuál?*
Which?	*¿Cuánto?*

Pronouns	Los pronombres
She	*Ellos*
He	*Ustedes*
We	*Él*
They	*Ella*
You guys	*Nosotros*

Numbers	Los números
10	*doce*
18	*treinta*
12	*diez*
15	*dieciocho*
30	*quince*

Days of the week	*Los días de la semana*
Monday	*miércoles*
Saturday	*domingo*
Sunday	*lunes*
Thursday	*sábado*
Wednesday	*jueves*

The weather	*El clima*
clear	*lluvia*
sun	*frío*
cold	*despejado*
snow	*nieve*
rain	*sol*

Feelings	*Los sentimientos*
well	*ocupado*
busy	*preocupado*
surprised	*bien*
angry	*sorprendido*
worried	*enojado*

Body parts	*Las partes del cuerpo*
back	*estómago*
throat	*espalda*
stomach	*dedo*
head	*pierna*
tooth	*cabeza*
leg	*rodilla*
eye	*cuello*
finger	*garganta*
neck	*ojo*
knee	*diente*

The family	*La familia*
father	*hijo*
sister	*esposa*
grandfather	*tío*
daughter	*hermana*
mother	*marido*
aunt	*abuelo*
uncle	*hija*
wife	*tía*
husband	*madre*
son	*padre*

Occupations	*Las ocupaciones*
chef	*bombero*
driver	*cajero*
student	*campesino*
gardener	*chofer*
cashier	*jardinero*
teacher	*estudiante*
plumber	*camarero*
waiter	*profesor*
farmer	*plomero*
firefighter	*cocinero*

Work	*El trabajo*
contract	*copiadora*
mail	*almacén*
strike	*fábrica*
product	*horario*
tool	*huelga*
copier	*correo*
factory	*herramienta*
schedule	*contrato*
warehouse	*producto*

Descriptions

Las descripciones

bad	*equivocado*
old	*guapo*
good	*viejo*
tall	*malo*
handsome	*blando*
inexpensive	*rubio*
empty	*barato*
soft	*bueno*
wrong	*vacío*
blond	*alto*

The house

La casa

closet	*escoba*
dryer	*trapeador*
rug	*espejo*
curtains	*cortinas*
mop	*alfombra*
washer	*plancha*
broom	*lavadora*
mirror	*sábanas*
iron	*secadora*
sheets	*ropero*

Rooms

Los cuartos

bedroom	*sala*
basement	*cocina*
kitchen	*dormitorio*
living room	*baño*
bathroom	*sótano*

Tools

Las herramientas

screwdriver	*escalera*
hose	*rastrillo*
saw	*destornillador*
rake	*manguera*
ladder	*serrucho*

The city	*La ciudad*
library	*supermercado*
post office	*escuela*
shoe store	*biblioteca*
church	*gasolinera*
supermarket	*zapatería*
pharmacy	*tienda*
bakery	*correo*
store	*farmacia*
gas station	*panadería*
school	*iglesia*

Transportation	*El transporte*
train	*avión*
boat	*autobús*
bicycle	*tren*
bus	*bote*
airplane	*bicicleta*

Animals	*Los animales*
duck	*caballo*
bird	*gato*
dog	*pájaro*
horse	*perro*
cat	*pato*
sheep	*vaca*
mouse	*puerco*
cow	*oveja*
pig	*ratón*

Food	*La comida*
steak	*pollo*
cookie	*helado*
bread	*galleta*
ice cream	*bistek*
turkey	*pastel*
lobster	*pan*
pie	*pavo*
candy	*langosta*
butter	*dulce*
chicken	*mantequilla*

Drinks	*Las bebidas*
milk shake	*leche*
wine	*jugo*
coffee	*batido*
juice	*café*
milk	*vino*

Clothing	*La ropa*
shorts	*camisa*
jacket	*medias*
hat	*calzoncillos*
shirt	*pantalones*
stockings	*sombrero*
raincoat	*guantes*
belt	*falda*
gloves	*impermeable*
skirt	*cinturón*
pants	*chaqueta*

Shopping	*Las compras*
bill	*cupón*
discount	*venta*
sale	*cuenta*
price	*descuento*
coupon	*precio*

Commands	*Mandatos*
Speak!	*¡Cállese!*
Go!	*¡Coma!*
Shut up!	*¡Escriba!*
Write!	*¡Vaya!*
Come!	*¡Hable!*
Eat!	*¡Espere!*
Wake up!	*¡Siéntese!*
Sit down!	*¡Despiértese!*
Wait!	*¡Agárrelo!*
Grab it!	*¡Venga!*

Verbs	*Los verbos*
open	*llorar*
cry	*vender*
carry	*abrir*
sell	*viajar*
travel	*llevar*

More verbs	*Más verbos*
save	*gritar*
rest	*celebrar*
wish	*ahorrar*
bet	*traducir*
celebrate	*buscar*
break	*descansar*
enjoy	*disfrutar*
yell	*quebrar*
translate	*desear*
look for	*apostar*

When?	*¿Cuándo?*
yesterday	*ayer*
before	*ahorita*
tomorrow	*a veces*
right now	*antes*
sometimes	*mañana*

Where?	*¿Dónde?*
outside	*hacia*
far	*arriba*
up	*afuera*
down	*lejos*
towards	*abajo*

Sports	*Los deportes*
team	*estadio*
coach	*partido*
stadium	*equipo*
practice	*entrenador*
match	*práctica*

Toys

blocks
skates
ball
kite
puzzle

Los juguetes

cometa
rompecabezas
cubos
pelota
patines

Things

pin
lock
box
deodorant
magazine
letter
tip
message
newspaper

Objetos

desodorante
periódico
alfiler
carta
caja
cerradura
revista
propina
mensaje

APPENDIX

Vocabulary/*Vocabulario*

Most of the words introduced in *Spanish for Gringos* can be found in the appendix. Action word forms such as the "Command Words" and specialty vocabulary such as "Traditional Foods," are not part of the appendix. Such terms are listed by category in the Table of Contents.

El and *la* are given only when you might be uncertain which is required (*la acción, el ángel*). Words that are the same or are both masculine and feminine are indicated by *el/la (el/la ayudante)*.

Note, too, that for convenience all verbs have been grouped under the "to" form on the English to Spanish side (*to allow, to answer, to arrange*, etc.).

You will also discover that some words may have multiple meanings or equivalents in the other language. However, the simple translations given here are general enough for basic conversational usage.

For more specific information, consult with a Spanish speaker, or refer to Barron's *Beginning Spanish Bilingual Dictionary*.

English—Spanish

a una, un
a little bit poco
a lot (many) muchos
a lot (much) mucho
a very little bit poquito
about acerca de
above encima
account cuenta
action la acción
actress la actriz
address la dirección
afterwards después
again otra vez
against contra
agency agencia
ahead adelante
AIDS el SIDA
air conditioning el aire acondicionado
airplane el avión
airport aeropuerto
all todo
almost casi
alone solo
along a lo largo de
already ya
also también
always siempre
American gringo, americano
and y
angel el ángel
angry enojado
animal el animal
anniversary aniversario
announcement anuncio
another otra, otro
ant hormiga
anxious ansioso
any cualquiera
anyone cualquiera persona
anywhere cualquiera parte
apartment apartamento
apple manzana
application la aplicación
appointment cita
April abril
apron el delantal
architect el/la arquitecto
area code código de área
around alrededor de

ashtray cenicero
asleep dormido
asphalt asfalto
assistant el asistente
astronaut el/la astronauta
at en
at last por fin
athlete el atleta
attic el desván
August agosto
aunt tía
auto insurance seguro de auto
available disponible
avenue avenida
awhile rato
baby el/la bebé
backward al revés
bag bolsa
bakery panadería
bald calvo
ball bola, pelota
balloon globo
banana plátano
bank banco
bar (drinking) cantina
barber shop peluquería
bargain ganga
baseball el béisbol
basement sótano
basic básico
basketball el básquetbol
bathrobe bata de baño
bathroom baño
bathtub tina
battery batería
bay bahía
bear (animal) oso
beautiful bello
because porque
bed cama
bedroom dormitorio
bee abeja
beer cerveza
before antes
behind detrás
bellboy el botones
belt el cinturón
besides además
between entre

Bible Biblia
bicycle bicicleta
big grande
bill cuenta
billion el billón
bird pájaro
birth nacimiento
birthday el cumpleaños
bitter amargo
black negro
blackboard el pizarrón
blame culpa
blanket cobija
bleach el blanqueador
blender licuadora
block (city) cuadra
blond rubio
blouse blusa
blue azul
boat barco
book libro
bookcase librero
boot bota
border frontera
bored aburrido
boss el jefe
both ambos
bottle botella
bottom fondo
bowling el boliche
box (container) caja
boxing boxeo
boyfriend novio
bracelet el brazalete
branch rama
brave valiente
bread el pan
brick ladrillo
bride novia
bridge el puente
briefcase el maletín
briefly brevemente
bright brillante
bring traer
broken roto
brooch el broche
broom escoba
broth caldo
brother hermano
brother-in-law cuñado

brown pardo, café
brush cepillo
bucket el balde
buddy compañero
building edificio
bus el autobús
bus stop parada de autobús
bush arbusto
but pero
butter mantequilla
cabbage repollo
cabinet el gabinete
cake torta
calendar calendario
camel camello
camera cámara
campgrounds campamento
can lata
candy el dulce
cap gorra
capital (letter) mayúscula
car carro
car lot el lote de carros
card (playing) carta
cardboard el cartón
carpenter carpintero
carrot zanahoria
cartoon caricatura
cashier cajero
cat gato
Catholic católico
cement cemento
cemetery cementerio
Central America Centroamérica
certain cierto
chain cadena
chair silla
chalk tiza
change cambio
chapter capítulo
check el cheque
checkers juego de damas
cheese queso
chef cocinero
cherry cereza
chess el ajedrez
chicken pollo
child niña, niño
chimney chimenea

China   China
Christian   cristiano
Christmas   la Navidad
church   iglesia
cigarette   cigarrillo
circus   circo
clarinet   el clarinete
clean   limpio
clever   listo
client   el cliente
climate   clima, tiempo
clock   el reloj
closed   cerrado
closet   ropero
cloth   tela
clothing   ropa
cloud   la nube
clown   payaso
coach   el entrenador
coast   costa
cockroach   cucaracha
coffee   el café
coffee pot   cafetera
coin   moneda
cold   frío
comb   el peine
command   mandato
communism   comunismo
community   la comunidad
computer   computadora
concert   concierto
conditioner (air)   el acondicionador
conference   conferencia
congratulations   felicitaciones
contract   contrato
conversation   la conversación
cook   cocinar
cooked   cocido
cookie   galleta
copier   copiadora
corn   el maíz
corner   esqina
correct   correcto
correctly   correctamente
couch   sofá
countryside   campo
couple   pareja, par
coupon   el cupón
court (sport)   cancha
court   la corte
cousin   primo
cow   vaca
coward   el cobarde
crab   cangrejo
crazy   loco
cream   crema
credit card   tarjeta de crédito
crime   el crimen
cross   la cruz
Cuba   Cuba
cup   taza
curtain   cortina
customs   aduana
cute   chulo
daily   diario
dance   el baile
dangerous   peligroso
dark   oscuro
dark-haired   moreno
darling   querido
date   fecha
daughter   hija
daughter-in-law   nuera
dawn   madrugada
day   el día
day before yesterday   anteayer
dead   muerto

death   la muerte
deer   venado
democracy   democracia
dentist   el dentista
deodorant   el desodorante
description   la descripción
desert   desierto
desk   escritorio
dessert   el postre
detergent   el detergente
detour   la desviación
devil   diablo
dialogue   diálogo
diamond   el diamante
dictionary   diccionario
diet   dieta
different   diferente
difficult   difícil
dining room   el comedor
dirt   tierra
dirty   sucio
discount   descuento
dish   el traste
distance   distancia
doctor   el/la médico
dog   perro
doll   muñeca
dollar   el dólar
domestic   doméstico
door   puerta
doorbell   el timbre
dot   punto
doubt   duda
down payment   el enganche
downtown   centro
downward   abajo
drawer   el cajón
dress   vestido
dresser   el tocador
drink   bebida
driver's license   licencia de chofer
drug   droga
drum   el tambor
dry   seco
dryer   secadora
duck   pato
dumb   tonto
during   mientras
dusk   el anochecer
dust   polvo
each   cada
early   temprano
earring   el arete
east   este
easy   fácil
easy chair   el sillón
effectively   efectivamente
egg   huevo
eight   ocho
eighteen   diez y ocho
eighty   ochenta
electric   eléctrico
electricity   la electricidad
elegant   elegante
elephant   el elefante
elevator   el elevador
eleven   once
emergency   emergencia
employee   empleado
empty   vacío
end   el fin
enemy   enemigo
engine   el motor
engineer   ingeniero
England   Inglaterra
English   inglés
enough   bastante
entrance   entrada

envelope   el sobre
every day   todos los días
everybody   todos, todo el mundo
everywhere   por todas partes
example   ejemplo
excellent   excelente
exercise   ejercicio
exit   salida
expensive   caro
experience   experiencia
factory   fábrica
faith   la fe
faithful   fiel
fall (season)   otoño
family   familia
famous   famoso
fantastic   fantástico
far   lejos
farm   finca
farmer   campesino
fat   gordo
father   el padre
father-in-law   suegro
fault   falta, culpa
favorite   favorito
fear   miedo
feather   pluma
February   febrero
fence   cerca
few   pocos
fiancé   novio
field   campo
fifteen   quince
fifty   cincuenta
fight   pleito
finally   finalmente, por fin
fireman   bombero
fireworks   fuegos artificiales
first   primer, primero
fish   pez, el
fish (cooked)   pescado
fisherman   el pescador
five   cinco
five hundred   quinientos
flag   bandera
flavor   el sabor
floor   piso
floor tile   baldosa
flower   la flor
fly (insect)   mosca
fog   neblina
following   siguiente
food   comida
for   para, por
for rent   se alquila
for sale   se vende
forest   el bosque
fork   el tenedor
form   forma
forward   adelante
four   cuatro
fourteen   catorce
forty   cuarenta
France   Francia
fresh   fresco
Friday   viernes
fried   frito
friend   amigo
friendly   amistoso
from   desde, de
frown   ceño
frying pan   la sartén
full   lleno
fun   la diversión
funny   chistoso
furious   furioso
furniture   los muebles
furniture store   mueblería

game   juego
gang   pandilla
garage   el garaje
garden   el jardín
gardener   el jardinero
garlic   ajo
gas station   gasolinera
gate   el portón
ghost   el fantasma
giraffe   jirafa
girlfriend   novia
glass   vidrio
glass (drinking)   vaso
glove   el guante
goat   chivo
God   Dios
gold   oro
good   bueno
good-bye   adiós
government   gobierno
grammar   gramática
grandchild   nieta, nieto
grandfather   abuelo
grandmother   abuela
grape   uva
grapefruit   toronja
grass   pasto, hierba
gray   gris
green   verde
green bean   judía verde
groom   novio
guide   el/la guía
guitar   guitarra
gum   el chicle
gymnasium   gimnasio
haircut   el corte de pelo
half   la mitad, medio
hallway   pasillo
ham   el jamón
hamburger   hamburguesa
hammer   martillo
hand   la mano
handkerchief   pañuelo
handsome   guapo
hanger   gancho
hard (to touch)   duro
hat   sombrero
he   él
health   la salud
heart   el corazón
heat   el calor
heating   la calefacción
heaven   cielo
helicopter   helicóptero
hell   infierno
hello   hola
helper   el/la ayudante
her   ella, su
here   acá, aquí
hers   suyo, suya
highway   carretera
hill   cerro
him   él
hippopotamus   hipopótamo
his   su, suyo, suya
Hispanic   hispánico, hispano
holy   santo
homework   tarea
honest   honesto
honey   la miel
hope   esperanza
horse   caballo
horseback riding   montar a caballo
hose   manguera
hospital   el hospital
hot   caliente
hot (spicy)   picante
hot dog   perro caliente

house casa
How many? ¿Cuántos?
How much? ¿Cuánto?
however sin embargo
hug abrazo
hundred cien
hundreds cientos
hunger el hambre
husband esposo
I yo
ice hielo
ice cream helado
if si
immediately inmediatamente
importance importancia
important importante
in en
in front of enfrente de
incorrect incorrecto
inexpensive barato
information la información
insect insecto
inside adentro
instrument instrumento
intelligent inteligente
interesting interesante
interview entrevista
introduction la introducción, la presentación
iron plancha
island isla
jacket chaqueta
jail la cárcel
January enero
Japan el Japón
jar frasco
jealous celoso
Jesus Christ Jesucristo
Jew judío
jewel joya
jewelry shop joyería
job trabajo
joke el chiste
juice jugo
July julio
June junio
jungle selva
just apenas
justice justicia
key la llave
kilogram (2.2 pounds) kilogramo
kilometer (5/8 of a mile) kilómetro
king el rey
kiss beso
kitchen cocina
kite el cometa
knapsack mochila
knife cuchillo
knot nudo
ladder escalera
lady dama, señora
lake lago
lamp lámpara
language el idioma, lengua
large grande
last último
last night anoche
late tarde
later luego
Latin latino
laughter risa
laundromat lavandería
law la ley
lawyer abogado
lazy perezoso
leaf hoja
left (direction) izquierda

lemon el limón
lemonade limonada
less menos
lesson la lección
letter (alphabet) letra
letter (mail) carta
lettuce lechuga
library biblioteca
license plate placa
lie (not true) mentira
life vida
light la luz
light (not dark) claro
likewise igualmente
lion el león
list lista
liter litro
living room sala
lobster langosta
lock cerradura
long largo
lost perdido
love el amor
lovely hermoso
lover el amante
low bajo
lowercase (letter) minúscula
luck la suerte
magazine revista
magic magia
magnificent magnífico
maid criada
mail correo
majority mayoría
makeup el maquillaje
man el hombre
manager el gerente
manner manera
map mapa
marble (toy) canica
March marzo
marriage matrimonio
marvelous maravilloso
match fósforo
maximum máximo
May mayo
meal comida
mean cruel
meaning significado
meat la carne
meat market carnicería
mechanic mecánico
medicine medicina
medium mediano
meeting junta
member miembro
message recado
meter metro
method método
Mexico México
middle medio
midnight la medianoche
milk la leche
milkshake batido de leche
million el millón
millionaire millonario
mine mío
minority minoría
minute minuto
miracle milagro
mirror espejo
Miss señorita
mister el señor
modern moderno
moment momento
Monday lunes
money dinero
monkey mono
month el mes

mop el trapeador
more más
mother la madre
motorcycle motocicleta
mouse el ratón
movie el cine
Mr. sr. (abr. for señor)
Mrs. sra. (abr. for señora)
mud lodo
museum museo
music música
musician músico
mustard mostaza
my mi, mis
nail clavo
name el nombre
napkin servilleta
narrow estrecho
nation la nación
nationality la nacionalidad
nature naturaleza
near cerca
necessary necesario
necklace el collar
needle aguja
neighborhood barrio
neither tampoco
nervous nervioso
net la red
never nunca
nevertheless sin embargo
perfume el perfume
news las noticias
newspaper periódico
next próximo, siguiente
nice simpático
nightmare pesadilla
nine nueve
nine hundred novecientos
nineteen diez y nueve
ninety noventa
no one nadie
none ninguna, ninguno
noon el mediodía
North America Norteamérica
notations apuntes
note nota
notebook cuaderno
nothing nada
notice la notificación
November noviembre
nowadays ahora
nowhere por ningún lado
number número
nurse enfermera
nut (food) la nuez
obvious obvio
ocean océano
October octubre
of de
of the del
offer oferta
office oficina
oil el aceite
old viejo
older mayor
on en
once una vez
one uno
onion cebolla
only sólo
open abierto
operation la operación
opposite contrario
or o
orange (fruit) naranja
orange (color) anaranjado
our nuestra(s), nuestro(s)
out of order descompuesto
outlet el enchufe

outside afuera
outskirts las afueras
over sobre
over there allá
overcoat abrigo
owner dueño
page página
pain el dolor
paint pintura
painter el pintor
pair par, pareja
pajamas piyama
pants los pantalones
paper el papel
parents los padres
park el parque
parking estacionamiento
party fiesta
passionate apasionado
passport el pasaporte
past pasado
payment pago
pea el guisante
peace la paz
pearl perla
pen pluma
pencil el lápiz
people la gente
pepper pimienta
perfectly perfectamente
perfume el perfume
person persona
pharmacy farmacia
philosophy filosofía
phone number número de teléfono
photo la foto
photography fotografía
pie el pastel
pig puerco
pillow almohada
pin el alfiler
pitcher cántaro
place el lugar, sitio
plant planta
plastic plástico
plate plato
playground patio de recreo
pleasant agradable
please por favor
pliers los alicates
plumber plomero
plumbing tubería
point punta
police policía
policy póliza
political party partido
politics política
pollution la contaminación
poor pobre
pork cerdo
possession la posesión
possible posible
post office (oficina de) correo
postcard tarjeta postal
pot olla
potato papa, patata
poverty pobreza
practice práctica
precious precioso
pregnant embarazada
presentation la presentación
president el presidente
pretty bonito
price precio
problem el problema
product producto
professional profesional
program programa

promise   promesa
pronunciation   la pronunciación
proud   orgulloso
public   público
punishment   castigo
purple   morado
purse   bolsa
puzzle   el rompecabezas
queen   reina
question   pregunta
quick   rápido
quickly   rápidamente
racket   raqueta
rain   lluvia
raincoat   el impermeable
rake   rastrillo
ranch   rancho
rat   rata
raw   crudo
razor   navaja
reading   lectura
ready   listo
reason   la razón
receipt   recibo
recipe   receta
recreation   recreo
red   rojo
red-headed   pelirrojo
refreshment   refresco
refrigerator   el refrigerador
relative   el pariente
religion   la religión
repair   la reparación
reservation   la reservación
respect   respeto
restaurant   el restaurante
restroom   sanitario
review   repaso
rhinoceros   el rinoceronte
ribbon   cinta
rice   el arroz
rich   rico
right (direction)   derecha
right now   ahora mismo
ring   anillo
ripe   maduro
river   río
road   camino
road sign   la señal
rock   roca
rocket   el cohete
romantic   romántico
room   la habitación
rotten   podrido
rough   áspero
rubber   goma
rug   alfombra
sail   navegar
saint   santo
salad   ensalada
sale   venta
salesperson   el vendedor, vendedora
salt   la sal
salty   salado
same   mismo
same to you   igualmente
sand   arena
sangria   sangría
Saturday   sábado
sauce   salsa
sausage   salchicha
saw   serrucho
saxophone   saxófono, el saxofón
scarf   bufanda
schedule   horario
school   escuela

scissors   las tijeras
screw   tornillo
screwdriver   el destornillador
sea   el/la mar
season   la estación
second   segundo
secretary   secretario
seed   semilla
seesaw   el sube y baja
sentence   la frase
September   septiembre
seven   siete
seven hundred   setecientos
seventeen   diez y siete
seventy   setenta
several   varios
sex   sexo
shampoo   el champú
she   ella
sheep   oveja
sheet (bed)   sábana
sheet (paper)   hoja
shirt   camisa
shoe   zapato
shoe store   zapatería
short (in height)   bajo
short (in length)   corto
shorts   los calzoncillos
shovel   pala
shower   ducha
shrimp   el camarón
shy   tímido
sickness   la enfermedad
side   lado
sidewalk   acera
signal light   semáforo
silver   plata
sincere   sincero
sincerely   sinceramente
single   soltero
sister   hermana
sister-in-law   cuñada
site   sitio, el lugar
six   seis
sixteen   diez y seis
sixty   sesenta
size   tamaño
skates   los patines
ski   esquiar
skirt   falda
skyscraper   el rascacielos
slippers   las pantuflas
slow   lento
slowly   despacio
small   chico
smile   sonrisa
smoke   humo
smooth   suave
snake   víbora
snow   la nieve
so   tan
soap   el jabón
soccer   el fútbol
social security   seguro social
socks   los calcetines
soft   blando
soldier   soldado
some   algún, algunos, algunas; uno(s), una(s)
someone   alguien
sometimes   a veces
somewhere   por algún lugar
son   hijo
son-in-law   yerno
soon   pronto
soul   el alma
sound   sonido
soup   sopa
sour   agrio

South America   Sudamérica
Spain   España
Spanish   español
special   especial
spend   gastar
spider   araña
spoon   cuchara
sport   el deporte
sports coat   saco
spring   primavera
stadium   estadio
stain   mancha
stairs   las escaleras
stamp   sello
station   la estación
steak   el bistec
step   paso
stereo   estéreo
stick   palo
still   aún
stone   piedra
store   tienda
stove   estufa
strange   extraño
strawberry   fresa
street   la calle
strike   huelga
strong   fuerte
structure   estructura
student   el estudiante
studious   aplicado
study   estudio
stupid   estúpido
subway   metro, (abr. for metropolitano)
suddenly   de repente
sugar   el/la azúcar
suit   el traje
suitcase   maleta
summer   verano
Sunday   domingo
sunset   puesta del sol
supermarket   supermercado
sure   seguro
surname   apellido
surprised   sorprendido
sweater   el suéter
sweatsuit   el traje de entrenamiento
sweet   dulce
sweethearts   los novios
swimming pool   piscina
swimsuit   el traje de baño
symbol   símbolo
T-shirt   camiseta
table   mesa
tablecloth   el mantel
tall   alto
tea   el té
teacher   maestro
team   equipo
tear (crying)   lágrima
telephone   teléfono
television   la televisión, el televisor
ten   diez
tennis   el tenis
terrible   terrible
terrific   terrífico
test   el examen
thanks   gracias
that   que
that (there)   esa, ese, eso
that (one)   ésa, ése
the (f)   la, las
the (m)   el, los
their   su, sus, suyos
theirs   suyo
theme   el tema

then   entonces
there   ahí
there is, there are   hay
therefore   por eso
these   estos, estas
these ones   éstos, éstas
they   ellos, ellas
thief   el ladrón
thin   flaco
thing   cosa
thirst   la sed
thirteen   trece
thirty   treinta
this   esto, esta, este
this one   ésta, éste
those   esos, esas
those (over there)   aquéllos, aquéllas
thousand   mil
thread   hilo
three   tres
throat   garganta
Thursday   jueves
ticket   boleto
tide   marea
tie   corbata
tiger   el tigre
time (hour)   hora
time   tiempo
tip   propina
tire (auto)   llanta
tired   cansado
to   a
to allow   dejar
to answer   contestar
to arrange   arreglar
to arrive   llegar
to attend   asistir
to avoid   evitar
to be   ser
to be (location and condition)   estar
to begin   empezar
to bet   apostar
to block   obstruir
to break   quebrar
to build   construir
to carry   llevar
to cast   lanzar, tirar
to catch   coger
to celebrate   celebrar
to chat   platicar
to check   revisar
to climb   subir
to close   cerrar
to comb one's hair   peinarse
to control   controlar
to court someone   pretender
to cry   llorar
to cut   cortar
to dance   bailar
to develop   desarrollar
to discuss   discutir
to do   hacer
to draw   dibujar
to dream   soñar
to drink   beber, tomar
to enjoy oneself   divertirse
to exit   salir
to find   encontrar
to finish   terminar
to fish   pescar
to fix   reparar
to float   flotar
to fly   volar
to forget   olvidar
to get dressed   vestirse
to give   dar
to guess   adivinar

to happen   suceder, pasar
to hate   odiar
to have   tener
to hit   golpear, pegar
to join   juntar
to kiss   besar
to learn   aprender
to leave   salir
to leave behind   dejar
to lend   prestar
to lie down   acostarse
to listen   escuchar
to look for   buscar
to lose   perder
to love   amar
to make   hacer
to make a call   hacer una llamada
to miss   faltar
to order   ordenar
to park   estacionar
to pass   pasar
to pay   pagar
to pitch   lanzar
to plant   plantar
to play *(a game)*   jugar
to play *(an instrument)* tocar
to pull   jalar
to push   empujar
to put   poner
to quit   renunciar
to raise oneself up   levantarse
to read   leer
to receive   recibir
to rest   descansar
to return   volver
to ride *(on the back of an animal)*   montar
to run   correr
to save *(keep)*   ahorrar
to say   decir
to sell   vender
to show   mostrar
to sing   cantar
to sit down   sentarse
to skate   patinar
to sleep   dormir
to smoke   fumar
to speak   hablar

to stick   pegar, adherir
to survive   sobrevivir
to swim   nadar
to take   tomar
to take advantage   aprovechar
to take away   quitar
to throw   tirar
to touch   tocar
to translate   traducir
to travel   viajar
to trust   confiar
to try   probar
to type   escribir a máquina
to visit   visitar
to walk   caminar
to wash   lavar
to watch   mirar
to weigh   pesar
to wish   desear
to work   trabajar
to yell   gritar
to yield   ceder
to the   al
toaster   tostador
today   hoy
together   juntos
toilet   excusado
tomorrow   mañana
tongue   lengua, el idioma
too, also   también
too much   demasiado
tool   herramienta
tourist   el/la turista
towards   hacia
towel   toalla
town   pueblo
traffic   tráfico
train   el tren
training   entrenamiento
trash can   el bote de basura
travel agency   agencia de viajes
treasure   tesoro
tree   el árbol
truck   el camión
truck driver   camionero
truth   la verdad
Tuesday   martes
turkey   pavo
twelve   doce

twenty   veinte
twin   gemelo
two   dos
typewriter   máquina de escribir
umbrella   el paraguas
underneath   debajo
underwear   ropa interior
United States   Estados Unidos
university   la universidad
until   hasta
upward   arriba
usually   usualmente
vacation   la vacación
vacuum cleaner   la aspiradora
valley   el valle
vase   florero
very   muy
very few   poquitos
very pretty   muy lindo
view   vista
violence   violencia
violent   violento
violin   el violín
vocabulary   vocabulario
voice   la voz
volleyball   el vóleibol
vote   voto
waiter   mesero
waitress   mesera
wallet   cartera
war   guerra
washbasin   lavabo
washer   la lavadora
watch   el reloj
water   el agua
wave   ola
we   nosotros, nosotras
weak   débil
weapon   el arma
weather   tiempo, el clima
wedding   boda
Wednesday   miércoles
week   semana
welcome   bienvenidos
well-mannered   educado
What?   ¿Qué?
When?   ¿Cuándo?
Where?   ¿Dónde?, ¿Adónde?
Which?   ¿Cuál?

white   blanco
Who?   ¿Quién?
Why?   ¿Por qué?
wide   ancho
wife   esposa
wild   salvaje
window   ventana
wine   vino
wine and fruit juice   sangría
winter   invierno
wire   el alambre
with   con
with me   conmigo
with you *(between friends, family)*   contigo
with him/her/them   consigo
without   sin
woman   la mujer
wood   madera
word   palabra
work   trabajo
world   mundo
writer   el escritor
written   escrito
wrong   equivocado
yard   patio
year   año
yellow   amarillo
yes   sí
yesterday   ayer
yet   todavía, aún
you *(between friends and family)*   tú
you   usted
you guys   ustedes
young   joven
young man   el joven
younger   menor
your *(between friends and family)*   tu
your   su
yours   suyo
yours *(between friends and family)*   tuyo
zebra   cebra
zero   cero
zip code   zona postal
zoo   zoológico

Spanish—English

a to
a lo largo de along
a veces sometimes
abajo downward
abeja bee
abierto open
abogado lawyer
abrazo hug
abrigo overcoat
abril April
abuela grandmother
abuelo grandfather
aburrido bored
acá here
acción, la action
aceite, el oil
acera sidewalk
acerca de about
acondicionador, el air conditioner
acostarse lie down
actríz, la actress
adelante ahead, forward
además besides
adentro inside
adherir to stick
adiós good-bye
adivinar guess
¿Adónde? Where?
aduana customs
aeropuerto airport
afuera outside
afueras, las outskirts
agencia agency
agencia de viajes travel agency
agosto August
agradable pleasant
agrio sour
agua, el water
aguja needle
ahí there
ahora nowadays
ahora mismo right now
ahorrar save
aire acondicionado, el air conditioning
ajedrez, el chess

ajo garlic
al to the
al revés backward
alambre, el wire
alfiler, el pin
alfombra rug
alguien someone
algún, algunos, algunas some
alicates, los pliers
alma, el soul
almohada pillow
alrededor (de) around
alto tall
allá over there
amante, el lover
amar to love
amargo bitter
amarillo yellow
ambos both
americano American
amigo friend
amistoso friendly
amor, el love
anaranjado orange *(color)*
ancho wide
ángel, el angel
anillo ring
animal, el animal
aniversario anniversary
anoche last night
anochecer, el dusk
anteayer day before yesterday
antes before
anuncio announcement
año year
ansioso anxious
apartamento apartment
apasionado passionate
apellido surname
apenas just
aplicación, la application
aplicado studious
apostar to bet
aprender to learn
aprovechar to take advantage
apuntes, los notations

aquéllas, aquéllos those *(over there)*
aquí here
araña spider
árbol, el tree
arbusto bush
arena sand
arete, el earring
arma, el weapon
arquitecto architect
arreglar to arrange
arriba upward
arroz, el rice
asfalto asphalt
asistente, el assistant
asistir attend
áspero rough
aspiradora vacuum cleaner
astronauta, el astronaut
atleta, el athlete
aún still, yet
autobús, el bus
avenida avenue
avión, el airplane
ayer yesterday
ayudante, el helper
azul blue
azúcar, el sugar
bahía bay
bailar to dance
baile, el dance
bajo short *(in height)*, low
balde, el bucket
baldosa floor tile
banco bank
bandera flag
baño bathroom
barato inexpensive
barco boat
barrio neighborhood
bastante enough
bata de baño bathrobe
batería battery
batido de leche milkshake
básico basic
básquetbol, el basketball
beber to drink
bebé, el baby

bebida drink
beisbol, el baseball
bello beautiful
besar to kiss
beso kiss
Biblia Bible
biblioteca library
bicicleta bicycle
bienvenidos welcome
billón, el billion
bistec, el steak
blanco white
blando soft
blanqueador, el bleach
blusa blouse
boda wedding
bola ball
boleto ticket
boliche, el bowling
bolsa bag, purse
bombero fireman
bonito pretty
bosque, el forest
bota boot
bote de basura, el trash can
botella bottle
botones, el bellboy
boxeo boxing
brazalete, el bracelet
brevemente briefly
brillante bright
broche, el brooch
bueno good
bufanda scarf
buscar look for
caballo horse
cada each
cadena chain
café, el coffee
cafetera coffee pot
caja box *(container)*
cajero cashier
cajón drawer
calcetines, los socks
caldo broth
calefacción, la heating
calendario calendar
caliente hot

calle, la   street
calor, el   heat
calvo   bald
calzoncillos, los   shorts
cama   bed
cámara   camera
camarón, el   shrimp
cambio   change
camello   camel
caminar   to walk
camino   road
camionero   truck driver
camión, el   truck
camisa   shirt
camiseta   T-shirt
campamento   campgrounds
campesino   farmer
campo   field, countryside
cancha   court (sport)
cangrejo   crab
canica   marble (toy)
cansado   tired
cantar   to sing
cántaro   pitcher
cantina   bar (drinking)
capítulo   chapter
la carcel   jail
caricatura   cartoon
carne, la   meat
carnicería   meat market
caro   expensive
carpintero   carpenter
carretera   highway
carro   car
carta   playing card, letter
   (mail)
cartera   wallet
cartón, el   cardboard
casa   house
casi   almost
castigo   punishment
católico   Catholic
catorce   fourteen
cebolla   onion
cebra   zebra
ceder   to yield
celebrar   to celebrate
celoso   jealous
cementerio   cemetery
cemento   cement
cenicero   ashtray
centro   downtown
Centroamérica   Central
   America
ceño   frown
cepillo   brush
cerca   near; fence
cerdo   pork
cereza   cherry
cero   zero
cerrado   closed
cerradura   lock
cerrar   to close
cerro   hill
cerveza   beer
champú, el   shampoo
chaqueta   jacket
cheque, el   check
chicle, el   gum
chico   small
chimenea   chimney
China   China
chiste, el   joke
chistoso   funny
chivo   goat
chulo   cute
cielo   heaven
cien   hundred
cientos   hundreds

cierto   certain
cigarrillo   cigarette
cinco   five
cincuenta   fifty
cine, el   movie
cinta   ribbon
cinturón, el   belt
circo   circus
cita   appointment
clarinete, el   clarinet
claro   light (not dark)
clavo   nail
cliente, el   client
clima, el   climate, weather
cobarde, el   coward
cobija   blanket
cocido   cooked
cocina   kitchen
cocinar   to cook
cocinero   chef
código del área   area code
coger   to catch
cohete, el   rocket
collar, el   necklace
comedor, el   dining room
cometa, la   kite
comida   food, meal
compañero   buddy
computadora   computer
comunidad, la   community
comunismo   communism
con   with
concierto   concert
conferencia   conference
confiar   to trust
conmigo   with me
consigo   with him/her/them
construir   build
contaminación, la   pollution
contestar   to answer
contigo   with you (between
   friends, family)
contra   against
contrario   opposite
contrato   contract
controlar   control
conversación, la   conversation
copiadora   copier
corazón, el   heart
corbata   tie
correctamente   correctly
correcto   correct
correo   mail, post office
correr   run
cortar   to cut
corte de pelo, el   haircut
corte, la   court
cortina   curtain
corto   short (in length)
cosa   thing
costa   coast
crema   cream
criada   maid
crimen, el   crime
cristiano   Christian
crudo   raw
cruel   mean
cruz   cross
cuaderno   notebook
cuadra   block (city)
¿Cuál?   Which?
cualquiera   any
cualquier parte   anywhere
cualquier persona   anyone
¿Cuándo?   When?
¿Cuánto?   How much?
¿Cuántos?   How many?
cuarenta   forty
cuatro   four

Cuba   Cuba
cucaracha   cockroach
cuchara   spoon
cuchillo   knife
cuenta   bill, account
culpa   fault, blame
cumpleaños, el   birthday
cuñada   sister-in-law
cuñado   brother-in-law
cupón, el   coupon
dama   lady
dar   to give
de   of, from
de repente   suddenly
debajo   underneath
débil   weak
decir   to say
dejar   to leave behind; to
   allow
del   of the
delantal, el   apron
demasiado   too much
democracia   democracy
dentista, el   dentist
deporte, el   sport
derecha   right (direction)
desarrollar   to develop
descansar   to rest
descompuesto   out of order,
   broken-down
descripción, la   description
descuento   discount
desde   from
desear   to wish
desierto   desert
desodorante, el   deodorant
despacio   slowly
después   afterwards
destornillador, el   screwdriver
desván, el   attic
desviación, la   detour
detergente, el   detergent
detrás   behind
día, el   day
diablo   devil
diálogo   dialogue
diamante, el   diamond
diario   daily
dibujar   to draw
diccionario   dictionary
dieta   diet
diez   ten
diez y nueve   nineteen
diez y ocho   eighteen
diez y seis   sixteen
diez y siete   seventeen
diferente   different
difícil   difficult
dinero   money
Dios   God
dirección, la   address
discutir   discuss
disponible   available
distancia   distance
diversión, la   fun
divertirse   to enjoy oneself
doce   twelve
dólar, el   dollar
dolor, el   pain
doméstico   domestic
domingo   Sunday
¿Dónde?   Where?
dormido   asleep
dormir   to sleep
dormitorio   bedroom
dos   two
droga   drug
ducha   shower
duda   doubt

dueño   owner
dulce   sweet
dulce, el   candy
duro   hard (to touch)
edificio   building
educado   well-mannered
efectivamente   effectively
ejemplo   example
ejercicio   exercise
él   he, him
el   the (m., sing.)
electricidad, la   electricity
eléctrico   electric
elefante, el   elephant
elegante   elegant
elevador, el   elevator
ella   she, her
ellos, ellas   they
embarasada   pregnant
emergencia   emergency
empezar   to begin
empleado   employee
empujar   to push
en   at, in, on
encima   above
encontrar   to find
enchufe, el   outlet
enemigo   enemy
enero   January
enfermedad, la   sickness
enfermera   nurse
enfrente de   in front of
enganche, el   down payment
enojado   angry
ensalada   salad
entonces   then
entrada   entrance
entre   between
entrenador, el   coach
entrenamiento   training
entrevista   interview
equipo   team
equivocado   wrong
esa, ese   that
ésa, ése   that one
esas, esos   those
ésas, ésos   those (there)
escalera   ladder
escaleras, las   stairs
escoba   broom
escribir a máquina   to type
escrito   written
escritor, el   writer
escritorio   desk
escuchar   to listen
escuela   school
eso   that
España   Spain
español   Spanish
especial   special
espejo   mirror
esperanza   hope
esposa   wife
esposo   husband
esquiar   ski
esquina, la   corner
esta, este   this
ésta, éste   this one
estación, la   season; station
estacionamiento, el   parking
estacionar   to park
estadio   stadium
Estados Unidos   United
   States
estar   to be (location and
   condition)
estas, estos   these
éstas, éstos   these ones
este   east

esto this
estrecho narrow
estructura structure
estudiante, el student
estudio study
estufa stove
estúpido stupid
evitar to avoid
examen, el test
excelente excellent
excusado toilet
experiencia experience
extraño strange
fábrica factory
fácil easy
falda skirt
falta fault
faltar to miss
familia family
famoso famous
fantasma, el ghost
fantástico fantastic
farmacia pharmacy
favorito favorite
fe, la faith
febrero February
fecha date
felicitaciones congratulations
fiel faithful
fiesta party
filosofía philosophy
fin, el end
finalmente finally, at last
finca farm
flaco thin
flor, la flower
florero vase
flotar to float
fondo bottom
forma form
fósforo match
fotografía photograph, photography
Francia France
frasco jar
frase, la sentence
fresa strawberry
fresco fresh
frío cold
frito fried
frontera border
fuegos artificiales fireworks
fuerte strong
fumar smoke
furioso furious
fútbol, el soccer
gabinete, el cabinet
galleta cookie
gancho hanger
ganga bargain
garaje, el garage
garganta throat
gasolinera gas station
gastar spend
gato cat
gemelo twin
gente, la people
gerente, el manager
gimnasio gymnasium
globo balloon
gobierno government
golpear to hit
goma rubber
gordo fat
gorra cap
gracias thanks
gramática grammar
grande big, large
gringo American

gris gray
gritar to yell
guante, el glove
guapo handsome
guerra war
guía, el/la guide
guisante, el pea
guitarra guitar
habitación, la room
hablar to speak
hacer to do, to make
hacer una llamada to make a call
hacia towards
hambre, el hunger
hamburguesa hamburger
hasta until
hay there is, there are
helado ice cream
helicóptero helicopter
hermana sister
hermano brother
hermoso lovely
herramienta tool
hielo ice
hija daughter
hijo son
hilo thread
hipopótamo hippopotamus
hispánico Hispanic
hispano Hispanic
hoja leaf, sheet (paper)
hola hello
hombre, el man
honesto honest
hora time (hour)
horario schedule
hormiga ant
hospital, el hospital
hoy today
huelga strike
huevo egg
humo smoke
idioma language; tongue
iglesia church
igualmente likewise, same to you
impermeable, el raincoat
importancia importance
importante important
incorrecto incorrect
infierno hell
información, la information
ingeniero engineer
Inglaterra England
inglés English
inmediatamente immediately
insecto insect
instrumento instrument
inteligente intelligent
interesante interesting
introducción, la introduction
invierno winter
isla island
izquierda left (direction)
jabón, el soap
jalar to pull
jamón, el ham
Japón, el Japan
jardín, el garden
jardinero gardener
jefe, el boss
Jesucristo Jesus Christ
jirafa giraffe
joya jewel
joyería jewelery shop
joven young, young man
judía verde green bean
judío Jew

juego game
juego de damas checkers
jueves Thursday
jugar to play (a game)
jugo juice
julio July
junio June
junta meeting
juntar to join
juntos together
justicia justice
kilogramo kilogram (2.2 pounds)
kilómetro kilometer (5/8 of a mile)
la, las the (f.)
lado side
ladrillo brick
ladrón, el thief
lago lake
lágrima tear (crying)
lámpara lamp
langosta lobster
lanzar to pitch, to cast
lápiz pencil
largo long
lata can
latino Latin
lavabo washbasin
lavadora washer
lavandería laundromat
lavar to wash
lección, la lesson
lectura reading
leche, la milk
lechuga lettuce
leer to read
lejos far
lengua tongue, language
lento slow
león, el lion
letra letter (alphabet)
levantarse to raise oneself up
ley, la law
librero bookcase
libro book
licencia de chófer driver's license
licuadora blender
limón, el lemon
limonada lemonade
limpio clean
lista list
listo ready; clever
litro liter
loco crazy
lodo mud
los the (m., pl.)
lote de carros, el car lot
luego later
lugar, el place, site
lunes Monday
luz, la light
llanta tire (auto)
llave, la key
llegar to arrive
lleno full
llevar to carry
llorar to cry
lluvia rain
madera wood
madre mother
madrugada dawn
maduro ripe
maestro teacher
magia magic
magnífico magnificent
maíz, el corn
maleta suitcase

maletín, el briefcase
mancha stain
mandato command
manera manner
manguera hose
mano, la hand
mantel, el tablecloth
mantequilla butter
manzana apple
mañana tomorrow
mapa, el map
maquillaje, el makeup
máquina de escribir typewriter
mar, el sea
maravilloso marvelous
marea tide
martes Tuesday
martillo hammer
marzo March
más more
matrimonio marriage
mayo May
mayor older
mayoría majority
mayúscula capital (letter)
máximo maximum
mecánico mechanic
mediano medium
medianoche midnight
medicina medicine
médico doctor
medio half, middle
mediodía, el noon
menor younger
menos less
mentira lie (not true)
mes, el month
mesa table
mesera waitress
mesero waiter
método method
metro (abr. for metropolitano) meter, subway
México Mexico
mi, mis my
miedo fear
miel, la honey
miembro member
mientras during
miércoles Wednesday
mil thousand
milagro miracle
millonario millionaire
millón, el million
minoría minority
minúscula lowercase (letter)
minuto minute
mío, mía mine
mirar to watch
mismo same
mitad, la half
mochila knapsack
moderno modern
momento moment
moneda coin
mono monkey
montar to ride (on the back of an animal)
montar a caballo horseback riding
morado purple
moreno dark-haired
mosca fly (insect)
mostaza mustard
mostrar to show
motocicleta motorcycle
motor, el engine
mucho a lot (much)

muchos a lot (many)
mueblería furniture store
muebles, los furniture
muerte, la death
muerto dead
mujer, la woman
mundo world
muñeca doll
museo museum
música music
músico musician
muy very
muy lindo very pretty
nacimiento birth
nación, la nation
nacionalidad, la nationality
nada nothing
nadar to swim
nadie no one
naranja orange (fruit)
naturaleza nature
navaja razor
navegar sail
Navidad, la Christmas
neblina fog
necesario necessary
negro black
nervioso nervous
nieta, nieto grandchild
nieve, la snow
ninguna, ninguno none
niña, niño child
nombre, el name
Norteamérica North America
norteamericano American (U.S.)
nosotras, nosotros we
nota note
noticias, las news
notificación, la notice
novecientos nine hundred
noventa ninety
novia girlfriend, bride
noviembre November
novio boyfriend, fiancé, groom
novios, los sweethearts
nube, la cloud
nudo knot
nuera daughter-in-law
nuestra(s), nuestro(s) our
nueve nine
nuez, la nut (food)
número number
número de teléfono phone number
nunca never
o or
obstruir to block
obvio obvious
océano ocean
octubre October
ochenta eighty
ocho eight
odiar to hate
oferta offer
oficina office
ola wave
olvidar forget
olla pot
once eleven
operación, la operation
ordenar to order
orgulloso proud
oro gold
oscuro dark
oso bear (animal)
otoño fall (season)
otra, otro another

otra vez again
oveja sheep
padre, el father
padres, los parents
pagar to pay
página page
pago payment
pájaro bird
pala shovel
palabra word
palo stick
pan, el bread
panadería bakery
pandilla gang
pantalones, los pants
pantuflas, las slippers
pañuelo handkerchief
papa potato
papel, el paper
par pair, couple
para for
parada de autobús bus stop
paraguas, el umbrella
pardo brown
pareja couple, pair
pariente, el relative
parque, el park
partido political party
pasado past
pasaporte, el passport
pasar to pass, to happen
pasillo hallway
paso step
pastel, el pie
pasto grass
patata potato
patinar to skate
patines, los skates
patio yard
patio de recreo playground
pato duck
pavo turkey
payaso clown
paz, la peace
pegar to hit, to stick
peinarse to comb one's hair
peine, el comb
peligroso dangerous
pelirrojo red-headed
pelota ball
peluquería barber shop
perder to lose
perdido lost
perezoso lazy
perfectamente perfectly
perfume, el perfume
periódico newspaper
perla pearl
pero but
perro dog
perro caliente hot dog
persona person
pesadilla nightmare
pesar to weigh
pescado fish (cooked)
pescador, el fisherman
pescar to fish
pez, el fish
picante hot (spicy)
piedra stone
pimienta pepper
pintor, el painter
pintura paint
piscina swimming pool
piso floor
piyama pajamas
pizarrón blackboard
placa license plate
plancha iron

planta plant
plantar to plant
plástico plastic
plata silver
plátano banana
platicar to chat
plato plate
pleito fight
plomero plumber
pluma feather; pen
pobre poor
pobreza poverty
poco a little bit
pocos few
podrido rotten
policía police (force and person)
política politics
póliza policy
polvo dust
pollo chicken
poner to put
poquito a very little bit
poquitos very few
por for
por algún lugar somewhere
por eso therefore
por favor please
por fin at last, finally
por ningún lado nowhere
¿Por qué? Why?
por todas partes everywhere
porque because
portón, el gate
posesión, la possession
posible possible
postre, el dessert
práctica practice
precio price
precioso precious
pregunta question
presentación, la presentation; introduction
presidente, el president
prestar to lend
pretender to court someone
primavera spring
primer, primero, primera first
primo cousin
probar try
problema, el problem
producto product
profesional professional
programa, el program
promesa promise
pronto soon
pronunciación, la pronunciation
propina tip
próximo next
público public
pueblo town
puente, el bridge
puerco pig
puerta door
puesta del sol sunset
punta point
punto dot
que that
¿Qué? What?
quebrar to break
querido darling
queso cheese
¿Quién? Who?
quince fifteen
quinientos five hundred
quitar to take away
rama branch

rancho ranch
rápidamente quickly
rápido quick
raqueta racket
rascacielos, el skyscraper
rastrillo rake
rata rat
rato awhile
ratón, el mouse
razón, la reason
recado message
receta recipe
recibir to receive
recibo receipt
recreo recreation
red, la net
refresco refreshment
refrigerador, el refrigerator
reina queen
religión, la religion
reloj, el clock, watch
renunciar to quit
reparación, la repair
reparar to fix
repaso review
repollo cabbage
reservación, la reservation
respeto respect
restaurante, el restaurant
revisar to check
revista magazine
rey, el king
rico rich
rinoceronte, el rhinoceros
río river
risa laughter
roca rock
rojo red
romántico romantic
rompecabezas, el puzzle
ropa clothing
ropa interior underwear
ropero closet
roto broken
rubio blond
sábado Saturday
sábana sheet (bed)
sabor, el flavor
saco sports coat
sal, la salt
sala living room
salado salty
salchicha sausage
salida exit
salir to leave, to exit
salsa sauce
salud, la health
salvaje wild
sangría sangria, wine and fruit juice
sanitario restroom
santo saint; holy
sartén, la frying pan
saxófono, el saxofón saxophone
se alquila for rent
se vende for sale
secadora dryer
seco dry
secretaria secretary
sed, la thirst
segundo second
seguro sure
seguro de auto auto insurance
seguro social social security
seis six
selva jungle
sello stamp

semáforo signal light
semana week
semilla seed
sentarse to sit down
señal, la road sign
señor, el mister, man
señora lady
señorita miss, young lady
septiembre September
ser to be
serrucho saw
servilleta napkin
sesenta sixty
setecientos seven hundred
setenta seventy
sexo sex
si if
sí yes
SIDA, el AIDS
siempre always
siete seven
significado meaning
siguiente following, next
silla chair
sillón, el easy chair
símbolo symbol
simpático nice
sin without
sin embargo however, nevertheless
sinceramente sincerely
sincero sincere
sitio site, place
sobre over, envelope
sobrevivir survive
sofá, el couch
soldado soldier
sola, solo alone
sólo only
soltero single
sombrero hat
sonido sound
sonrisa smile
soñar to dream
soñoliento sleepy
sopa soup
sorprendido surprised
sótano basement

Sr. (*abr. for* **señor**) Mr.
Sra. (*abr. for* **señora**) Mrs.
Srta. (*abr. for* **señorita**) Miss
su your; his; her; their
suave smooth
sube y baja, el seesaw
subir to climb
suceder to happen
sucio dirty
Sudamérica South America
suegro, el father-in-law
sueño dream
suerte, la luck
suéter, el sweater
supermercado supermarket
suyo his, hers, yours, theirs
tamaño, el size
también too, also
tambor, el drum
tampoco neither
tan so
tarde late
tarea homework
tarjeta de crédito credit card
tarjeta postal postcard
taza cup
té, el tea
tela cloth
teléfono telephone
televisión, la television
televisor, el television
tema, el theme
temprano early
tenedor, el fork
tener to have
tenis, el tennis
terminar to finish
terrible terrible
terrífico terrific
tesoro treasure
tía aunt
tío uncle
tiempo time; weather
tienda store
tierra dirt
tigre, el tiger
tijeras, las scissors
timbre, el doorbell

tímido shy
tina bathtub
tirar to throw, to cast
tiza chalk
toalla towel
tocador, el dresser
tocar to touch; to play (an instrument)
todavía yet
todo all
todo el mundo everybody
todos everybody
todos los días every day
tomar take; drink
tonto dumb
tornillo screw
toronja grapefruit
torta cake
tostador, el toaster
trabajar to work
trabajo work, job
traducir to translate
traer to bring
tráfico traffic
traje, el suit
traje de baño, el swimsuit
traje de entrenamiento, el sweatsuit
trapeador, el mop
traste, el dish
trece thirteen
treinta thirty
tren, el train
tres three
tú you (*between friends and family*)
tu your (*between friends and family*)
tubería plumbing
turista, el/la tourist
tuyo yours
último last
una vez once
una, un a
unas, unos some
universidad, la university
uno one
usted you

ustedes you guys
usualmente usually
uva grape
vaca cow
vacación, la vacation
vacío empty
valiente brave
valle, el valley
varios several
vaso glass (*drinking*)
veinte twenty
venado deer
vendedor, el salesperson
vender to sell
venta sale
ventana window
verano summer
verdad, la truth
verde green
vestido dress
vestirse to get dressed
viajar to travel
víbora snake
vida life
vidrio glass
viejo old
viernes Friday
vino wine
violencia violence
violento violent
violín, el violin
visitar to visit
vista view
vocabulario vocabulary
volar to fly
vóleibol, el volleyball
volver to return
voto vote
voz, la voice
y and
ya already
yerno son-in-law
yo I
zanahoria carrot
zapatería shoe store
zapato shoe
zona postal zip code
zoológico zoo

English-Spanish Verb Lists

accept, to **aceptar**
add, to **agregar, añadir**
advance, to **avanzar**
advise, to **recomendar**
agree, to **convenir**
allow, to **permitir**
answer, to **contestar**
arrive, to **llegar**
ask for, to **pedir**
ask, to **preguntar**
assist, to **atender**
attend, to **asistir**
be able to, to **poder**
be born, to **nacer**
be, to **estar, ser**
beg, to **suplicar**
begin, to **comenzar, empezar**
believe, to **creer**
belong, to **pertenecer**
bend, to **doblar**
bite, to **morder**
boil, to **hervir**
break, to **quebrar, romper**
breathe, to **respirar**

bring, to **traer**
build, to **construir**
buy, to **comprar**
call, to **llamar**
carry, to **llevar**
catch, to **atrapar**
change, to **cambiar**
charge, to **cargar**
choose, to **escoger**
clean, to **limpiar**
climb, to **subir**
close, to **cerrar**
collect, to **coleccionar**
come, to **venir**
confuse, to **confundir**
consider, to **considerar**
contain, to **contener**
convince, to **convencer**
cook, to **cocinar**
correct, to **corregir**
cost, to **costar**
count, to **contar**
cover, to **cubrir, tapar**
crash, to **chocar**

cross, to **cruzar, atravesar**
cry, to **llorar**
cut, to **cortar**
dance, to **bailar**
decide, to **decidir**
deliver, to **entregar**
deny, to **negar**
describe, to **describir**
desire, to **desear**
destroy, to **destruir**
die, to **morir**
dig, to **excavar**
discover, to **descubrir**
discuss, to **discutir**
divide, to **dividir**
do, to **hacer**
draw, to **dibujar**
dream, to **soñar**
drink, to **beber, tomar**
drive, to **manejar**
dry, to **secar**
earn, to **ganar**
eat, to **comer**
empty, to **vaciar**

end, to **acabar, terminar**
enter, to **entrar**
examine, to **examinar**
explain, to **explicar**
fall, to **caer**
fear, to **temer**
feed, to **alimentar**
feel, to **sentir**
fight, to **pelear**
fill, to **llenar**
find, to **encontrar**
find out, to **averiguar**
fish, to **pescar**
fit, to **caber**
fix, to **componer**
fly, to **volar**
follow, to **seguir**
forget, to **olvidar**
forgive, to **perdonar**
freeze, to **congelar**
get down, to **bajar**
get near, to **acercar**
get, to **obtener**
give, to **dar**

go, to **ir**
go out, to **salir**
greet, to **saludar**
grind, to **moler**
grow, to **crecer**
hang, to **colgar**
happen, to **suceder**
hate, to **odiar**
have, to **tener**
hear, to **oír**
help, to **ayudar**
hide, to **esconder**
hire, to **contratar**
hit, to **pegar**
hold, to **sostener**
hug, to **abrazar**
hunt, to **cazar**
hurt, to **doler**
imagine, to **imaginar**
include, to **incluir**
injure, to **herir**
insert, to **meter**
insist, to **insistir**
install, to **instalar**
interpret, to **interpretar**
invest, to **invertir**
judge, to **juzgar**
jump, to **saltar**
keep, to **guardar**
kick, to **patear**
kiss, to **besar**
know (someone), to **conocer**
know (something), to **saber**
lay, to **colocar**
lead, to **guiar**
learn, to **aprender**
leave, to **salir**
lend, to **prestar**
let, to **permitir**
lie, to **mentir**
lift, to **levantar**
light, to **encender**

like, to **gustar**
listen, to **escuchar**
live, to **vivir**
look, to **mirar**
loosen, to **soltar**
lose, to **perder**
love, to **amar**
maintain, to **mantener**
make, to **hacer**
mark, to **marcar**
mean, to **significar**
measure, to **medir**
meet, to **encontrar**
move, to **mover**
need, to **necesitar**
notify, to **notificar**
obey, to **obedecer**
obtain, to **obtener**
offer, to **ofrecer**
open, to **abrir**
oppose, to **oponer**
order, to **ordenar**
owe, to **deber**
park, to **estacionar**
pay, to **pagar**
permit, to **permitir**
persist, to **persistir**
pick up, to **recoger**
plant, to **plantar**
play, to **jugar**
plug in, to **enchufar**
polish, to **bruñir, pulir**
practice, to **practicar**
pray, to **rezar**
prefer, to **preferir**
prepare, to **preparar**
prevent, to **prevenir**
promise, to **prometer**
pronounce, to **pronunciar**
protect, to **proteger**
prove, to **probar**
pull, to **jalar**

push, to **empujar**
put, to **poner**
quit, to **renunciar**
rain, to **llover**
reach, to **alcanzar**
read, to **leer**
receive, to **recibir**
recognize, to **reconocer**
recommend, to **recomendar**
reduce, to **reducir**
refer, to **referir**
remember, to **recordar**
rent, to **alquilar**
repair, to **reparar**
repeat, to **repetir**
require, to **requirir**
rest, to **descansar**
retire, to **retirar**
return, to **devolver**
ride, to **montar**
run, to **correr**
sail, to **navegar**
save, to **ahorrar**
say, to **decir**
scratch, to **rascar**
search, to **buscar**
see, to **ver**
seem, to **parecer**
select, to **seleccionar**
sell, to **vender**
send, to **enviar, mandar**
serve, to **servir**
set, to **colocar**
sew, to **coser**
shake, to **sacudir**
share, to **compartir**
shoot, to **disparar**
shout, to **gritar**
show, to **mostrar**
sing, to **cantar**
skate, to **patinar**
sleep, to **dormir**

smoke, to **fumar**
snow, to **nevar**
speak, to **hablar**
spend, to **gastar**
stay, to **quedar**
stir, to **batir, revolver**
study, to **estudiar**
subtract, to **restar**
sweep, to **barrer**
swim, to **nadar**
take care of, to **cuidar**
take out, to **sacar**
take, to **tomar**
talk, to **hablar**
teach, to **enseñar**
tell, to **decir**
thank, to **agradecer**
think, to **pensar**
threaten, to **amenazar**
throw, to **tirar**
touch, to **tocar**
translate, to **traducir**
travel, to **viajar**
try, to **tratar**
turn around, to **voltear**
turn off, to **apagar**
turn on, to **prender, encender**
understand, to **comprender, entender**
use, to **usar**
visit, to **visitar**
vote, to **votar**
walk, to **caminar, andar**
want, to **querer**
wash, to **lavar**
wear, to **llevar**
win, to **ganar**
wish, to **desear**
work, to **trabajar**
worry, to **preocupar**
write, to **escribir**

The Reflexives

bathe, to **bañarse**
become, to **hacerse**
brush, to **cepillarse**
change address, to **mudarse**
comb, to **peinarse**
complain, to **quejarse**
dress, to **vestirse**
fall asleep, to **dormirse**
fall down, to **caerse**

forget about, to **olvidarse**
get angry, to **enojarse**
get better, to **mejorarse**
get sick, to **enfermarse**
get married, to **casarse**
get ready, to **arreglarse**
get up, to **levantarse**
have a good time, to **divertirse**

hurry up, to **darse prisa**
leave, to **irse**
lie down, to **acostarse**
make a mistake, to **equivocarse**
make fun of, to **burlarse**
put on, to **ponerse**
realize, to **darse cuenta de**
remember, to **acordarse**

remove, to **quitarse**
shave, to **afeitarse**
sit down, to **sentarse**
stand up, to **pararse**
stay, to **quedarse**
wake up, to **despertarse**
wash, to **lavarse**
worry about, to **preocuparse**

Personal Success Chart

Date   *Mi experiencia*

_____

                 I used a greeting!

_____

                 I understood my Spanish-speaking neighbor!

_____

_____

_____

_____

_____

_____

NOTES